The Coffee Culture
***

Delicious Tropical
Fruits

Directed and Edited by:
BENJAMIN VILLEGAS

Studio Photography Direction:
Liliana Villegas

Studio Photography:
Eliaju Ben Ephraïm

Exterior Photography:
Jorge Eduardo Arango

Maps and Illustrations:
Hernán Cuervo

Design:
Liliana Villegas
Benjamín Villegas

Art and Production Supervisor:
Mercedes Cedeño

Research and Indexes:
Guillermo Vera

Production Assistant:
Germán Vallejo

Translated from the Spanish by:
Pedro Shaio and Andrea de Villamizar

Copyright
© 1990 Villegas Editores
Carrera 13 N⁰ 33-74 Oficina 303
Postal address: Apartado Aéreo 7427
Bogotá, Colombia.
Telephone: 245 77 88 - 285 18 37
Telefax: (91) 28816 96.

First Edition 1990

ISBN. Complete work 953-9133-28-4
ISBN. 958-9138-60-8

Printed in Japan by
Toppan Printing Co., Ltd.

The publication of this book has been possible thanks
to the generous support of the:
CORPORACION FINANCIERA DE CALDAS S.A.
(CALDAS FINANCIAL CORPORATION),
the FEDERACION NACIONAL DE CAFETEROS DE COLOMBIA
(COLOMBIAN COFFEE-GROWERS' FEDERATION),
and the FONDO DE PROMOCION DE EXPORTACIONES -
PROEXPO -(EXPORT PROMOTION FUND)

The author especially wishes to thank the following people
whose help made this book possible:
Gloria Jaramillo de Vélez, Ligia González de Villegas,
Sofía Salazar, Lidy Gómez de Villegas,
Hilda Villegas de Gómez, Estela Upegui,
Clara Hoyos de Arbeláez, Clara Lucía Salazar de Villegas,
Alba María Jaramillo de Villegas, Ofelia Serna,
Polidoro Pinto, Jaime Cañón, Rosalía Castro
Rafael Mejía, Mónica Jaramillo.

For Marcelo, Sofía and Francisco.

LILIANA VILLEGAS

Delicious Tropical *Fruits*

Villegas editores

Contents

And the Lord God planted a garden in Eden in the East; and there He put the man whom He had formed, and out of the ground the Lord God made to grow every tree that is pleasant to the sight and good for food.

(Genesis, Chapter 2, Verses 8-9)

*N*othing in the world is quite as exquisite, satisfying and digestive as fresh fruit. Rich in vitamins, salts, minerals and fiber and with a seemingly infinite variety of colors, aromas and flavors, fruit is the ideal complement to any meal.

Fruits involve all of the senses. They charm us with fragrant perfumes and nuances of sweetness that defy definition; with indescribable flavors at once sweet and sour; with mild and liquid consistencies. Their shapes, made even more interesting by their changing colors and textures - velvety, wrinkled or menacingly thorny - promise vital food, a cure for ills, the quelling of thirst and hunger and a great source of energy.

One of the most delicious ways to eat fruits is *au naturel:* section or break them open, or else simply sink your teeth into them. Fruits make a simple and easy snack, pleasing at any time of day or night. Some can be eaten skin and all, and consumed this way are even more nutritious and healthy. Experts recommend eating fresh fruit at the beginning of each day to cleanse and prime the organism. For every fruit, there is a right moment and proper ritual, because each variety can delight us in its own way.

Fruit can be used in a great many forms in cooking: from cooked simply in syrup to the most sophisticated fruit sauces that enrich or set off the most exquisite dishes. With fruit, any salad can acquire an unmistakable touch of flavor; as to liqueurs, in addition to acquiring flavor, they are enhanced by the colors of different fruits. Nothing could be more elegant than serving fruit salad in a bowl made from a halved shell or surprising guests with an exotic fruit soup.

Traditionally, many women's beauty secrets include fruits in the preparation of a large number of treatment masks to relax, beautify and tone the skin. Certain fruits are also used as natural medicines, or are included in their preparation.

A fruit bowl makes an infallibly beautiful centerpiece for the dining room table. To create an effortless though perishable masterpiece, select ripe and beautifully colored fruits, wash them and perhaps polish them. The fruit can be chosen and combined virtually at random, for no matter how you build your bowl, a symphony of shapes and colors will result.

A fruit's aspect is a good indicator of its quality. Select those which look full, have good coloring and smell delicious. Generally speaking, a wrinkled fruit, a moldy one or one whose juice oozes is not of good quality. When choosing, compare the size of the fruit to its weight. A large-sized fruit that weighs little will be dry and therefore not succulent. Ripe fruit quickly loses its nutrient values. Except for fruit that only matures on the branch, it is best to select fruits that are not quite ripe, then store them in a fresh, cool place until just ready to eat.

Using fruit in an ever increasing number and variety of dishes will better the nutritional value of our diet while providing us with a visual feast at the table.

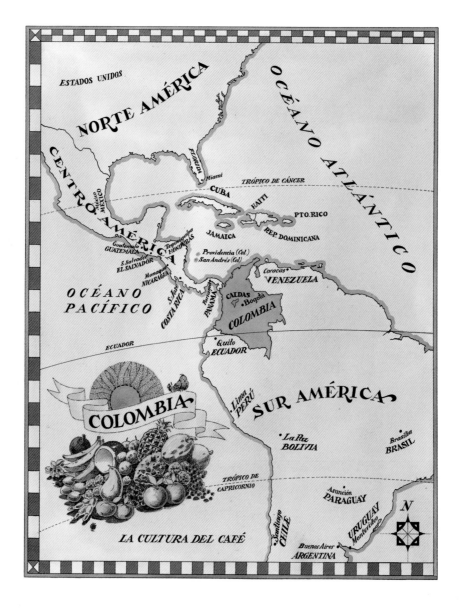

$\mathcal{O}$ld Caldas, Colombia's principal coffee-growing region, is also one of the country's richest fruit-producing areas. Its orchards produce a great variety of prime quality and truly exquisite tropical fruits. The region's epicenter is the snowcapped Ruiz Volcano, which rises majestically to over 17,000 feet above sea level.

Where the mountains are born, life too is born. The purest waters flow down from the heights in tiny streams - some ice-cold and others steaming hot - wearing deep paths in the rock. The raging peak is also the source of the ash which fertilizes the surrounding mountainous area. Thus, though the volcano does at times erupt in destructive fire; it nourishes and renews the earth.

To journey down from the highlands which surround the Ruiz to the fully tropical Magdalena and Cauca River Valleys is to experience in the space of a few hours, almost all of the soil-types and climates possible on this planet - a startling synthesis of the world's microcosms. Even the high-altitude mist forests of the colder climes harbor many fruit species: blackberries, curubas, lulos, tamarillos, uchuvas, chachafrutos, feijoas, granadillas and figs. Some grow wild and others are under cultivation, in a landscape graced by residual primary forests where ancient cedars and oaks survive, their trunks and branches, hung with parasites, orchids and anturiums amidst ferns and many other local plants. This is also the habitat of the tall and severely elegant wax palm, Colombia's national tree.

In the temperate climates banana fronds, the swaying crests of the bamboo stands and the carbonero trees, interspersed with fine hardwoods, surround well-organized coffee plantations. In the warm, aromatic air, one's senses relax and expand. The intensely cultivated land fairly bursts with melons, pitaya, pineapples, papayas, guavas, oranges and avocados. These slopes make up the mountain heartland of the tropical Andes, immensely rich in plant and animal species, a veritable earthly paradise capable of integrating many species into a single, profuse scenario.

Finally, the way opens up and we reach the hot lowlands. Here the mountains give way to small plains divided by ample rivers which become more and more impressive as they flow north to the Caribbean. The green of the nearby landscape sharpens and then bursts into millions of vibrant tones. Watermelons, mangos, limes, guanábanas, cherimoyas and tamarinds grow near the coconut and cohune palms which join the ceibas and royal palms in providing blessed shade to men and beasts.

For generations, the mountainous region of Old Caldas has lived close to nature, to agriculture, to a natural and healthy environment refreshed by fruit. The presence of fruit trees in the landscape has been permanent, though it was more noticeable before the newer varieties of coffee were introduced. The traditional varieties needed the shade provided by fruit trees, hardwood and flowering trees. These in turn provided complementary income, lumber and fresh fruit for everyone.

Fruits have always been the pride of these lands and an integral part of their culture. Today as ever, the marketplaces and busy street corners of the towns are full of fruit vendors. As ever, the enticing kitchens give off delicate aromas. Fruit is the single ingredient which has inspired the greatest variety of concoctions and the most original recipes as well as the most ingenious culinary techniques. After-dinner conversations frequently lead to lively discussions; friends compare one fruit to another, describing flavors or sensations in a cartography of fruit whereby each locality is identified by a product or a recipe.

Looking at the potential for fruit production, we are now presented with an unequaled opportunity for ecological reordering, with incalculable economic opportunity and with the delicious prospect of making our diet more pleasant and healthy.

Now that fruit cultivation is once again an important economic activity in this and other regions of Colombia, preserving and indeed reestablishing the ecosystem in its diversity is a priority task, for this is the only sensible manner to avoid devastation, pests, deforestation, erosion, water loss and contamination. The local tradition of mixed forests has established an excellent bio-ethical precedent which integrates the naturalist's criteria of being aware of and responsible for the endangered planet.

Hopefully, fruit production will become one of Colombia's greatest assets as well as remaining an essential part of our heritage.

Recipe index

Pitaya

Acanthocereus pitajaya (Jacq.) Dugand.

$\mathscr{P}$itaya is of the cactus family, thus it can withstand drought. It is a tropical fruit, originally from the American continent, found from the Florida coasts to southern Peru. The term pitaya comes from Haiti and means "scaled fruit". In Colombia it can be cultivated from sea level to nearly 5,000 ft. above sea level but its ideal habitat is around 2,200 ft.

There are approximately 18 varieties of pitaya. One of them, when ripe, is yellow on the outside and has a transparent white pulp with a multitude of tiny black seeds. Another when ripe has red flesh and pulp. Though it is more handsome to look at, it has less flavor than its yellow cousin. There are also native varieties growing in the wild. Flowering begins with the rainy season and the principal harvesting is done in accordance with each region's rainfall.

The pitaya is an exquisite fruit, eaten primarily as a fresh fruit but also used in cocktails and beverages. The plant can be found in gardens as an ornamental species not only because it is always green but also thanks to its fragrant and lovely flowers.

As all fruits, it contains a high percentage of water. The pitaya, in addition to carbohydrates, contains phosphorus, calcium and ascorbic acid. Many are afraid of eating pitaya for fear of diarrhea, but this should not put people off because

Alder forest in Manizales, Caldas.

the fruit helps clean out the system. Several chemical products have been identified and isolated from both the green and the ripe fruit as well as from its aerial parts, with definite applications in the pharmaceutical industry.

It is practically impossible to find a perfect pitaya since the scale-like points of the fruit turn black when lightly touched. These blackened points, however, do not damage the fruit because its outer skin is very resistant. The pitaya should be yellow and firm but not hard. When it starts to shrivel, it is overripe. It can be stored in a fresh place for a few days, but if you wish to keep it longer, it should be refrigerated.

100 g. of edible fruit contain:	
Water	85.4 g.
Protein	0.4 g.
Fat	0.1 g.
Carbohydrates	13.2 g.
Fiber	0.5 g.
Ash	0.4 g.
Calcium	10 mg.
Phosphorus	16 mg.
Iron	0.3 mg.
Vitamin A	0 I.U.
Thiamine	0.03 mg.
Riboflavin	0.04 mg.
Niacin	0.2 mg.
Ascorbic Acid	4 mg.
Calories	50 cal.

Feijoa

Acca sellowiana (Berg.) Burret.

The feijoa is originally from South America. It owes its name to Don José de Silva Feija, botanist and director of the Museum of Natural History in Madrid during the Colonial period. Sellowiana honors Friedrich Sellow, a German botanist who explored Brazil during the 19th century.

The feijoa flourishes at altitudes from 5,500 to 7,400 ft. above sea level and, once beyond the five year mark, the plant produces permanently. There are two varieties: Triumph and Mammoth.

This fruit conserves its aroma whether fresh or cooked. It can be used in fruit or green salads, but sparingly: its flavor is strong and could overpower other ingredients. It mixes well with papaya, bananas, oranges and strawberries. It is delicious in any kind of dessert, mousse, ice cream or juice. Although its skin is edible and tangy, many prefer to peel it to obtain a smoother texture. Its pleasing and seductive aroma and flavor have made it quite popular.

New Zealand is the world's primary exporter of feijoas. Experiments in cultivating the fruit have been conducted in California since the turn of the century, but the feijoa continues to be referred to as a new fruit. In reality, the feijoa was relegated to a secondary position for many years and the trees were considered valuable only as ornaments, especially in the colder climates. Today there is no doubt as to this fruit's magnificent qualities and it is thought to have great potential.

If the fruit is not ripe, it is rather tart, but once ripe it is sweet. It should be firm to the touch, with a full-bodied aroma and without insect bites or black spots. To accelerate its ripening, it can be wrapped in newspaper. Once ripe it can be kept in the refrigerator for two or three days. It can also be puréed and frozen.

100 g. of edible fruit contain:	
Water	82.6 g.
Protein	0.9 g.
Fat	0.0 g.
Carbohydrates	11.9 g.
Fiber	1.0 g.
Ash	3.6 g.
Calcium	36 mg.
Phosphorus	16 mg.
Iron	0.7 mg.
Vitamin A	0 I.U.
Thiamine	0.04 mg.
Riboflavin	00.4 mg.
Niacin	1.0 mg.
Ascorbic Acid	4 mg.
Calories	46 cal.

Cherimoya

Annona cherimolia (Lam.) Mill.

100 g. of edible fruit contain:	
Water	77.1 g.
Protein	1.9 g.
Fat	0.1 g.
Carbohydrates	18.2 g.
Fiber	2.0 g.
Ash	0.7 g.
Calcium	32 mg.
Phosphorus	37 mg.
Iron	0.5 mg.
Vitamin A	0 I.U.
Thiamine	0.10 mg.
Riboflavin	0.14 mg.
Niacin	0.9 mg.
Ascorbic Acid	5 mg.
Calories	73 cal.

The cherimoya originated in Colombia and Peru. Its cultivation has extended to the Antilles, Guyana and Venezuela, always in mid-range climates, at altitudes of between 4,100 and 5,000 ft.

There are different varieties, according to the characteristics of the fruit. Among the best known are the so-called Concha Lisa or smooth shell, Bronceada or bronzed, Terciopelo or velvet and Pícula varieties, this last being perhaps the most pleasing to the palate.

Because of its exquisite flavor, the fruit is usually eaten fresh, chilled or at room temperature. It should be served in the shell as a final course; half a cherimoya per person is sufficient.

For many people, the cherimoya is the world's most delicious fruit because of its sweet smell and delicate texture. Haenke called it "nature's masterpiece and true delight". It really is a refreshing and digestive fruit.

Known for its aroma, a cherimoya must be ripe when picked, for it does not mature well once removed from the tree. Its skin should be dark green, smooth to the touch but not too soft and without hard spots.

A cherimoya should not be stored in the refrigerator, but it can be chilled for a while before serving, making it even more delectable.

Mango

Mangifera indica L.

Native to East Asia, the mango spread from there to all other tropical countries on the earth.

In Colombia, varieties exist that were developed more than three hundred years ago. Some of these, very popular in present-day markets, are mangas, particularly good for juice, also the huge and succulent red mangoes and the small, truly delectable sugar mangoes.

There are two groups of varieties: the Indian, considered to be noble and made up of more than 1000 varieties; and the Indochinese, considered wild. The Mulgoba variety is the most representative of the Indian group, while the Camboya is the best known of the Indochinese varieties. Each group possesses particular characteristics: while the Indian specimens are usually rounded, red, purple or yellow in color and sweet flavored with little acid; the Indochinese, called mangas, present an elongated rather than broad shape, greenish yellow color and a sweet flavor with a touch of tartness. The ideal altitude for growing mangoes is between 1,650 to 2,200 ft.

In addition to being a fruit with an incomparable flavor, the mango provides mankind with carbohydrates, vitamins and minerals. It is eaten fresh but also in juices, salads, ice creams, marmalades, mousses, soufflés and the famed mango chutney, excellent with bread, vegetables, meats and poultry.

Mangoes possess a high percentage of water, sugar and fiber. They are also rich in absorbable iron, calcium and phosphorus. Industrially, they are processed into pulp, juice as well as pickled and canned fruit.

From the seed of the mango - ground, washed to remove all traces of tannin and dried - a flour is obtained which compares favorably in nutritional value to rice. It is used quite successfully in animal feeds.

When choosing a mango, check the following: its skin should adhere well to the pulp, be thin and firm to the touch. There should be no hard or dark spots nor holes or blemishes from insect damage, improper handling or disease.

Mangoes are delicate, they can be stored for only a few days in a cool place. It is best to keep them refrigerated.

100 g. of edible fruit contain:	
Water	81.8 g.
Protein	0.5 g.
Fat	0.1 g.
Carbohydrates	16.4 g.
Fiber	0.7 g.
Ash	0.5 g.
Calcium	10 mg.
Phosphorus	14 mg.
Iron	0.4 mg.
Vitamin A	1,100 I.U.
Thiamine	0.04 mg.
Riboflavin	0.07 mg.
Niacin	0.4 mg.
Ascorbic Acid	80 mg.
Calories	58 cal.

Lulo

Solanum quitoense Lam.

100 g. of edible fruit contain:	
Water	92.5 g.
Protein	0.6 g.
Fat	0.1 g.
Carbohydrate	5.7 g.
Fiber	0.3 g.
Ash	0.8 g.
Calcium	8 mg.
Phosphorus	12 mg.
Iron	0.6 mg.
Vitamin A	600 I.U.
Thiamine	0.04 mg.
Riboflavin	0.04 mg.
Niacin	1.5 mg.
Ascorbic Acid	25 mg.
Calories	23 cal.

*I*n Colombia, in warm and medium climates up to 5,200 ft. above sea level, the lulo grows almost wild. It is called lulo or naranjilla and produces fruit all year round.

Except by those who like tart, sour fruits, most people prefer lulo in juices, ice creams and other mixtures that contain a good amount of sugar. Lulo always provides amazing and interesting results.

In addition to water content, which is proportionately quite high, lulo also contains proteins, phosphorus, niacin, ascorbic acid, calcium and iron.

Perhaps lulo juice is one of the most delightful, providing energy and quenching thirst; it should be drunk chilled.

The fruit should be of a good size. It can be used either green or ripe but if it is too green, there will be no juice. The ideal fruit should be hard and free of holes, black spots or other damages.

Lulos should be stored in a cool place or in the refrigerator.

Sapodilla

Matisia cordata H. & B.

*T*his fruit is native to the Colombian Andes. It grows wild but is also cultivated in hot and temperate zones in altitudes up to 4,100 ft.

The sapodilla or zapote is a most agreeable fruit with a rather subtle flavor. It is difficult to eat because it is extremely fibrous, but for that same reason it is an excellent source of digestible fiber, which works to clean out the intestines. The color of the exotic sapodilla is especially beautiful and characteristic.

The leaves on the tree are used in the Colombian Pacific shore for weaving wonderful hats. The oil from the seeds is used by Mexican Indians to treat hair and to improve the flavor of chocolate.

When selecting a sapodilla, it is advisable to choose one that is hard and no larger than the palm of one's hand. There are sapodillas up to 1 1/2 ft, in diameter but the smaller versions are more succulent, whereas the larger ones tend to be insipid.

It is a most difficult fruit to store because it deteriorates in a very few days.

100 g. of edible fruit contain:	
Water	85.1 g.
Protein	1.1 g.
Fat	0.1 g.
Carbohydrates	12.4 g.
Fiber	0.6 g.
Ash	0.7 g.
Calcium	25 mg.
Phosphorus	32 mg.
Iron	1.4 mg
Vitamin A	1,000 I.U.
Thiamine	0.05 mg.
Riboflavin	0.09 mg.
Niacin	0.4 mg.
Ascorbic Acid	20 mg.
Calories	49 cal.

cherimoyas with yoghurt and müesli.

serves 2

1 cherimoya
Yoghurt
Müesli

Slice the cherimoya in half and spoon out some of the pulp from the fruit's center. Remove the pits, cut the pulp into small pieces and put it back into the shell. Now cover the fruit with yoghurt and müesli. The cherimoya can be refrigerated one hour before serving.

cherimoya nougat.

1 lb. cherimoya pulp
1 1/2 lbs. sugar
3 tablespoons lime juice
Wafers (round and thin,
about 8 inches in diameter)
Raisins
Orange and lime peels,
blanched
Almonds
Cohune nuts

Place the fruit pulp, mixed with the sugar and the lime juice, in a heavy pot and cook over medium heat, stirring constantly to avoid sticking until obtaining the consistency of heavy syrup (p. 80). Allow to cool. Chop the raisins, the peels and the almonds finely and mix them with the fruit. To construct the nougat, spread a layer of wafers and then one of the fruit and nut mixture, pressing gently as you go along and leaving a layer of wafers on top. Cool for 4 hours in the refrigerator and then cut into chunks.

Variations: The cherimoya can be replaced with sour-sop or guanábana. Other ingredients that may be used are peanuts, pistachio nuts, crystallized fruits, etc. Instead of using wafers, "cherimoya cheese" can be made: using a hand whisk, beat 2 egg whites until stiff. Add two tablespoons of sugar and whisk until glossy.

Mix in the fruit and nuts, spread evenly in a moistened pan and cool.

feijoa mousse.

serves 6

1 lb. feijoas
3 tablespoons lime juice
1/2 cup sugar
3 envelopes gelatine
(unsweetened and unflavored)
4 eggs
Almond oil

Soak the gelatine in cold water and then dissolve it in a small amount of hot water. Remove about half of the peel from the feijoas, cover them with water and blend the fruit with the lime juice. Strain, mix with the gelatine and cool for 10 minutes. Now blend again or whisk by hand. In another bowl, beat the egg whites until stiff, then add the sugar and the yolks. Place this in a pan which has been lightly coated with sweet almond oil and fold the feijoas into the mixture. Cool until it sets and decorate with feijoa flowers. This mousse can be served with the following sauce:

feijoa sauce 1.

6 peeled feijoas
2 cups water
1 cup sugar
Juice of 1/2 lime

Blend the feijoas with the water and then strain. In a pot, simmer the fruit with the sugar until obtaining the consistency of light syrup (p. 80) and then add the lime juice.

light orange mousse with feijoa sauce.

2 cups orange juice
1 lb. sugar
2 1/2 envelopes gelatine
4 egg whites beaten until stiff

Boil the sugar in 1 cup of water to make a medium syrup (p. 80). Soak the gelatine in cold water and then stir it into the syrup. Allow the syrup to cool, add the orange juice and then blend until smooth. Fold in the egg whites and then spread the mix evenly in a lightly oiled pan. Place it in the refrigerator to cool. When the mousse has set, it can be removed from the pan and covered with the following sauce:

feijoa sauce 2.

12 feijoas
1 cup honey
1 cup water
1 cup orange juice

Blend half of the unpeeled feijoas and slice the remaining 6 finely. Leave the honey and the fruit to simmer in the water until the feijoas look glossy and you have medium syrup (p. 80).

This sauce can be served as a light dessert in its own right. It is also delicious over ice cream.

pitaya on ice.

The pitaya is as exotic as it is
exquisite. Its delicate taste
invites us to eat it without
further ado. It looks inviting
and refreshing on a bed of
crushed ice, either in slices or
simply cut in half and eaten
with a small spoon.

mango soufflé.

serves 2

3/4 cup mango purée
(1 large mango)
1 tablespoon lime juice
3 egg whites
Salt and pepper to taste

Pre-heat the oven to 200°.
Lightly oil a soufflé pan and
sprinkle it with sugar. In a
pot, simmer the mango
pureé, sugar, lime juice and a
pinch of salt. Stir constantly
until this mixture is smooth
and heavy, then remove from
heat. Beat the egg whites
until stiff but not too dry and
then fold them into the hot
fruit. Now spread this mix
evenly in the pan and leave
at 350° for 30 minutes.
Serve immediately. The
following sauce can be added:

green mango sauce.

1 cup sugar
1 cup unsweetened yoghurt
2 egg whites
1/2 cup cream
2 peeled green mangoes

Blend the pulp of 1 mango
with the yoghurt and half of
the sugar. Separately, beat
the egg whites until stiff,
adding the remaining sugar.
In another bowl, whip the
cream and pour in the egg
whites and lastly the mango.
Chop the other mango finely
and add to the sauce.

small pitaya pastries.

serves 2

8 small puff pastries (p. 109)
Feijoa sauce
l peeled and sliced pitaya

Slice the pastries horizontally and place a piece of pitaya between the halves. Pour the sauce onto a dish and then place the pastries on it.

feijoa sauce 3.

1 cup sugar
1 cup unsweetened yoghurt
Juice and grated peel
of 2 limes
2 egg whites
1/2 cup heavy cream
4 large feijoas, partially
peeled

Blend the feijoas with the lime juice, the lime peel, half of the sugar and the yoghurt. Beat the egg whites until stiff, adding the remaining sugar. In a separate bowl, place an ice cube in the cream and then whip it until wrinkles appear on its surface. Add the egg whites and the feijoa mixture to the cream and place this in the refrigerator to cool. The sauce should be lightly hand-whisked before serving.

mango gelatine.

2 cups strained mango juice
1 lb. sugar
1 cup water
6 envelopes unflavored
gelatine
4 eggs

Prepare a heavy syrup (p. 80) with sugar and water. Soften the gelatine in a small quantity of cold water and then mix it into the syrup. Remove the pot from the heat, add the mango juice and blend until smooth. Beat the eggs, mix them in and spread this evenly in a lightly oiled pan. Cool and allow to set before removing.

mango chutney.

3 lbs. mangos, peeled and
chopped
2 lbs. sugar
1/2 lb. raisins
10 cloves garlic
4 cloves
2 sweet red peppers, finely
chopped
2 teaspoons salt
3 cups fruit vinegar

Set the sugar aside. Simmer
the remaining ingredients
until the red pepper and the
mango soften, then add the
sugar and leave at medium
heat for 40 min. Allow the
chutney to cool and then
preserve it in sterilized jars
(pp. 168-9).

Chutney is a delicious sweet
and sour condiment that
enhances curry or pork
dishes. It can also be used as
a marmalade

chicken salad with pitaya.

serves 4

3 pitayas, peeled and sliced
Lettuce
2 chicken breasts, stewed and diced
1/4 cup homemade avocado mayonnaise (p. 142)

Mix the chicken with the mayonnaise, and place this on a bed of lettuce leaves on each plate. Garnish with slices of pitaya.

This is an ideal dish for a light luncheon or tea

chicken breast medallions à la Mariquiteña.

serves 6

6 chicken breasts
3 tablespoons flour
1 tablespoon Worcestershire
sauce
3 cups oil
1/2 lb. yellow cheese
Salt and pepper to taste

Bone the chicken and beat it with a mallet to soften it. Marinate it in the sauce, salt and pepper. Roll up each section of chicken around a piece of yellow cheese and fasten the ends with a wooden toothpick. Roll each piece in the flour and fry it in hot oil. Then cut the chicken into medallions and serve with the following hot sauce:

mango sauce.

12 small ripe mangos
1 tablespoon butter
1/4 cup sugar
1 1/2 tablespoons cornflour
dissolved in 1/4 cup water

Peel and pit the mangos. Heat the pulp until the fruit comes to a boil, stirring with a wooden spoon. Add the cornflour, butter and sugar, and allow to simmer for 10 minutes.

A perfect entré when you are short of time and need something special.

lulo pie.

serves 8

pie pastry.

1 1/2 cups crumbled crackers
6 tablespoons melted butter
1 1/2 teaspoons powdered
cinammon (optional)

Mix all the ingredients, place the dough in a pie pan and press against the bottom and sides with your fingers. Keep the pan in the refrigerator while you prepare the filling.

This is an exquisite dessert, easy and quick, appropriate for lunch or informal dinners.

lulo cream.

1 large can condensed milk
1 cup concentrated lulo juice
1 tablespoon lime juice
3 tablespoons sugar
3 eggs, separated
1/2 teaspoon cream of tartar

Beat the yolks until creamy and pale, then add the condensed milk, lime juice and lulo concentrate. Heat and stir until the cream thickens, then remove from heat. Beat the egg whites until stiff, mixing in the cream of tartar and the sugar. Gently fold the egg whites into the cream and fruit mixture, then pour the filling into the pan and leave in the refrigerator until it sets.

lulo sherbet.

serves 6

6 lulos
Sugar to taste
1 small cup triple sec

Prepare lulo juice and sweeten it to taste, then pour in the liqueur and freeze. Take the juice out of the freezer a few times and blend at low speed to prevent crystallization and to obtain a creamy consistency. Serve in champagne glasses garnished with candied rose petals.

candied rose petals.

Rose petals in several colors
1 tablespoon powdered gum arabic
2 tablespoons rose water
Granulated sugar

Sprinkle a flat pan with granulated sugar which has been sifted several times. In a cup, mix the gum arabic with the rose water. Brush the petals with this mixture and place them in the pan, sprinkling more sugar over them. Now place the petals on a fine metal grille and leave in a barely warm oven until completely dry.

sapodilla juice.

This is a delicious fruit that may be eaten fresh when cut open like a flower, as in the photograph.
The pulp can be used to make a refreshing and filling juice or sherbet.
Cut open the fruit, peel and section it. Place the pulp in a strainer and slowly add water or milk, stirring and mashing with a wooden spoon until the pits are quite free of fruit pulp. Blend the juice, sweeten to taste and serve with crushed ice in round cups.

Flowering cámbulos and an old coffee plantation, Risaralda, Caldas.

Pineapple

Ananas sativus Shultz.

The pineapple, so called because the Spaniards saw it as a huge pine nut, is native to Brazil and Paraguay. Its name in Guaraní is "ananá". The men who arrived with Columbus to Guadalupe in 1493 must have been quite surprised when they cut open this thorny, forbidding fruit, only to find a bright yellow inside that looked like edible sunshine - withal a sweet, aromatic fruit, but one that also bites back. By the 17th century the pineapple had already established itself in the majority of the world's tropical regions, for it is a popular fruit that satisfies both thirst and hunger.

Approximately 80 varieties of pineapple are known, the majority of which extract water from the atmosphere, thus allowing the plant to thrive in arid climates up to 3,100 ft. above sea level. The best-known varieties are the Water, Perolera, Cayena, Piamba, and Huitota.

Ripe pineapple contains a high percentage of sugar. Furthermore, it contains a substance called bromelin, an enzyme which aids in the digestion of proteins, making pineapple a good aid to digestion. Paradoxically, for it is basically an acid fruit, pineapple also helps to combat stomach acidity by producing base salts.

Pineapple is very good in fruit salads, and as a juice it is pure delight. This fruit is used in many recipes to provide a tasty contrast to meats. As a filling in sweet dishes, cakes and tarts, in ice cream and sherbets, pineapple is exceptional. The core of the pineapple, also nutritious, is used in the preparation of sweets and candies.

Pineapple rind steeped in water with unrefined sugar produces a fine vinegar or astringent drink called guarapo. If this is allowed to ferment for a few days it turns into a diuretic beverage that has a most pleasant flavor.

If the rind is conserved in water, it becomes mucilaginous and can be used as hair styling gel or for dressing the tails and manes of show horses. It is also the basis for the following native remedy for gallstones: one glass of pineapple juice mixed with half a glass of olive oil; drink half at night and the other half the following morning. The leaves of the fruit are useful: they provide a fine, glossy white fiber that can be braided and woven into strong ropes and cloth.

The fruit should be completely healthy. Any imperfection is enough reason for rejecting it. Furthermore, the color should look half-ripe; the fruit should not be hard; it should smell sweet and the "eyes" should be large.

100 g. of edible fruit contain:	
Water	85.1 g.
Protein	0.4 g.
Fat	0.1 g.
Carbohydrates	13.5 g.
Fiber	0.5 g.
Ash	0.4 g.
Calcium	21 mg.
Phosphorus	10 mg.
Iron	0.4 mg.
Vitamin A	0 I.U.
Thiamine	0.09 mg.
Riboflavin	0.03 mg.
Niacin	0.2 mg.
Ascorbic Acid	12 mg.
Calories	51 cal.

Papaya

Carica papaya L.

It is an American fruit that comes from warm and temperate climates up to 1,600 meters above sea level. It has extended to many countries and latitudes and is one of the basic foods in the American tropics.

Seventy one species of papaya are distributed among four genus. All are originally from the tropics of the American continent, especially in the humid valleys of the Pacific coasts of Colombia and Ecuador, with the noted exception of "Cyclicomorfa" papaya which comes from Africa. Each species bears fruits of a different size from small papayas that are perfect for one serving to some enormous ones that measure half a meter in length and 30 centimeters in diameter.

It can be eaten fresh, sprinkled with a few drops of lemon or orange juice. It is also very good in fruit salads or as the basis for a juice which is as refreshing as it is substantial. A slice of papaya and a cup of coffee in the morning will provide freshness and energy to start the day. Some people believe that salt improves the flavor.

Unripened papaya contains papain, an enzyme which breaks down protein, helps digestion and tenderizes meat. Papain is also obtained from the latex that oozes out when incisions are made in the skin of the fruit. It is a naturally diuretic fruit and purifies the digestive system. A one day papaya diet is excellent for cleansing the system and provides the organism with a beneficial rest.

The skin of the papaya, with a bit of fruit stuck to it is an excellent hydrating agent for the skin, even for the face. Leave it on for a few minutes, then wash well with soap and water.

The seeds of the ripe papaya can be used to season foods if they are cleaned and then ground finely. Cover them the first day with boiling vinegar, enough to moisten the ground seeds; repeat the process the next day. With this treatment they acquire a flavor similar to that of watercress and a spiciness much like mustard.

The stage of ripeness and color are fundamental when selecting a papaya. For immediate serving, the papaya must be firm to the touch but not hard. The skin must be yellowish and of course it must be in good condition. Since it is a delicate fruit, it must be harvested carefully to avoid bruising. To prevent the fruit from drying out too quickly, the harvester must make sure that a small portion of the stem remains on the fruit when it is picked.

The papaya is one of the few fruits that can be bought green and left to ripen at home. To accelerate the process, small incisions should be made on the surface of the fruit so that the latex drains out and then it can be placed in sunshine for a little while. Papayas should be stored in a cool place or in the refrigerator at 13 degrees Centigrade, the ideal temperature for retarding ripening without damaging the fruit.

Temperatures below 10 degrees Centigrade do not allow the fruit to ripen.

100 g. edible fruit contain:	
Water	90.0 g.
Protein	0.5 g.
Fat	0.1 g.
Carbohydrates	8.1 g.
Fiber	0.8 g.
Ash	0.5 g.
Calcium	25 mg.
Phosphorus	12 mg.
Iron	0.3 mg.
Vitamin A	700 I.U.
Thiamine	0.03 mg.
Riboflavin	0.02 mg.
Niacin	0.3 mg.
Ascorbic Acid	75 mg.
Calories	30 cal.

Melon

Cucumis melo L.

The cucumber family of fruits (cucurbitaceae) propagated thousands of years ago throughout the Asian and African continents. Their cultivation is so ancient that a Cornucopia painted on a glass manufactured in Alexandria shows melons beside other fruits. The Greeks cultivated melons in the 3rd century B.C. and in Europe they were very popular in the 15th century. In the latter part of the 1600's, the melon was introduced to the Antilles and from there it spread to all of tropical America, for the fruit grows best in hot climates.

There are different types of melons. The commercial varieties are divided into reticulates and cataloupes. Among the first group, "Golden Delight", "Gold Cup" and "Hale's Best" are outstanding.

Leaders in the second group are the "Verde Trepador", "Charentais" and "Bellegrade".

Usually the melon is an aromatic, exquisite and nutritious fruit. It quenches thirst and irrigates the organism. A slice is always welcome at the breakfast table, at lunch-time as a snack or else an appetizer or as a dessert after dinner. Like most fruits, melons affect the system gently, acting in this case as a diuretic and tranquillizer.

In general terms, melons should have a pleasant aroma; the ideal color depends on the variety of the melon but they should not be picked very green because they do not ripen well off the vine.

To know whether a melon is sufficiently ripe, gently press the ends of fruit. If it is ripe, these points will be slightly softer than the rest of the fruit. It should be stored in a cool place or in the refrigerator.

100 g. of edible fruit contain:	
Water	96.6 g.
Protein	0.3 g.
Fat	0.0 g.
Carbohydrates	4.1 g.
Fiber	0.5 g.
Ash	0.5 g.
Calcium	13 mg.
Phosphorus	14 mg.
Iron	0.2 mg.
Vitamin A	130 I.U.
Thiamine	0.02 mg.
Riboflavin	0.01 mg.
Niacin	0.4 mg.
Ascorbic Acid	22 mg.
Calories	16 cal.

Watermelon

Citrullus vulgaris Schrader

Watermelons are thought to be a native African fruit, but that opinion is not unanimous. Surviving bas reliefs and sculptures indicate that watermelons were grown in the Nile River valley in the time of the pharaohs. However, Linnaeus, the Swedish botanist, located their origin in central Italy and others have stated that they come from India. Whatever their origin, they grow well in hot climates.

The color of the pulp is generally red, although, according to the species, it can have several hues. In the past, yellow-meat watermelons were cultivated. The quite numerous seeds are dark, blackish, spotted or completely black.

There are three basic types: the spherical ones, among which the most outstanding are the "Sugar Baby" - a relatively small melon with a dark green rind and very sweet red meat - the "Black Diamond", which can weigh up to 20 kilos and the "Mijako", which has a pale green-striped rind. Then come the huge oval-shaped spotted melons like the "Charleston Gray", "Klondike Striped" and "Dixie Queen"; and lastly, the smaller oval melons that weigh between 5 and 6 kilos, such as the "Sweetmeat", a very fragrant and sweet fruit especially appreciated because it is almost seedless.

Those who enjoy eating watermelon need have no fear of

gaining weight, because most of this fruit is simply water.

Watermelon is excellent for quenching thirst and its delicately-flavored juice, lightly chilled, does not require further sweetening. It is also very good in fruit salads. The rind imakes a wonderful pickle.

A watermelon should be hard, firm and well-formed. One side should be of a deeper color than the rest. Once opened, it is easy to determine the quality of the fruit; the pulp should be juicy, of a deep pink to red color, without white spots and with dark, lustrous seeds.

This fruit should be stored in a fresh place; it also responds well to refrigeration. It is important to remember that a watermelon can only be kept for a very short time after opening it because it quickly spoils and becomes poisonous.

100 g. of edible fruit contain:	
Water	95.7 g.
Protein	0.4 g.
Fat	0.0 g.
Carbohydrates	3.4 g.
Fiber	0.3 g.
Ash	0.2 g.
Calcium	4 mg.
Phosphorus	5 mg.
Iron	0.3 mg.
Vitamin A	300 I.U.
Thiamine	0.02 mg.
Riboflavin	0.01 mg.
Niacin	0.1 mg.
Ascorbic Acid	7 mg.
Calories	12 cal.

Guanábana

Annona muricata L.

The guanábana, known as soursop, originated in the American tropics.

When the Spanish conquistadors arrived, they found that it was consumed by the natives of all the countries from Peru to Mexico. Some affirm that the guanábana comes from Central America, particularly Guatemala or southern Mexico. It flourishes in the tropics from sea level to 5,000 ft. above sea level.

There are no definitive varieties but the fleshy thorns, size, the shape of the leaves and the height of the tree do differentiate the trees.

This fruit is delectable and has abundant pulp. A guanábana is delicious to bite into and provides an intriguing mixture of sweet and sour. It can be eaten naturally, perhaps chilled, and is the basis of delicious desserts like meringues, mousses and ice creams.

A guanábana should be a little soft to the touch. If it has hard spots it will not ripen uniformly. The fruit spoils rapidly if it is bruised or merely opened; in either case it should be used immediately.

Once ripened, guanábana pulp can be stored in the following manner: remove the seeds, mix six parts of pulp with one part sugar and store in sealed plastic bags in the refrigerator or freezer. On the other hand, if you want to speed up maturation, place the fruit in a

bowl filled with water, making certain that the stem is submerged.

100 g. of edible fruit contain:	
Water	83.4 g.
Protein	1.1 g.
Fat	0.2 g.
Carbohydrates	13.0 g.
Fiber	1.6 g.
Ash	0.7 g.
Calcium	22 mg.
Phosphorus	28 mg.
Iron	0.4 mg.
Vitamin A	0 I.U.
Thiamine	0.04 mg.
Riboflavin	0.07 mg.
Niacin	0.9 mg.
Ascorbic Acid	25 mg.
Calories	52 cal.

guanábana ice cream.

2 cups guanábana pulp
13 oz. cream
1 can condensed milk
Juice of 1/2 lime
3 egg whites beaten until stiff
Grated lime peel

Set aside the egg whites and blend the remaining ingredients. Place the mix in a mold and freeze for 20 minutes. Then blend again and fold in the egg whites with a wooden spoon. Pour the ice cream into individual serving cups, garnish with a sprinkling of lime peel and freeze. Remove 10 minutes before serving.

watermelon juice.

serves 8

1 watermelon
Juice of 1 lime
Sugar to taste
1/2 bottle soda water

Slice the watermelon lengthwise somewhat above the mid-point in order to obtain a usable shell. Spoon out some of the pulp into small balls, keep these cool and add before serving. Then extract all the pink pulp, remove the seeds and blend the pulp with the sugar, soda water and lime juice. Freeze this for 1 hour. Immediately before serving, pour the juice into the watermelon.

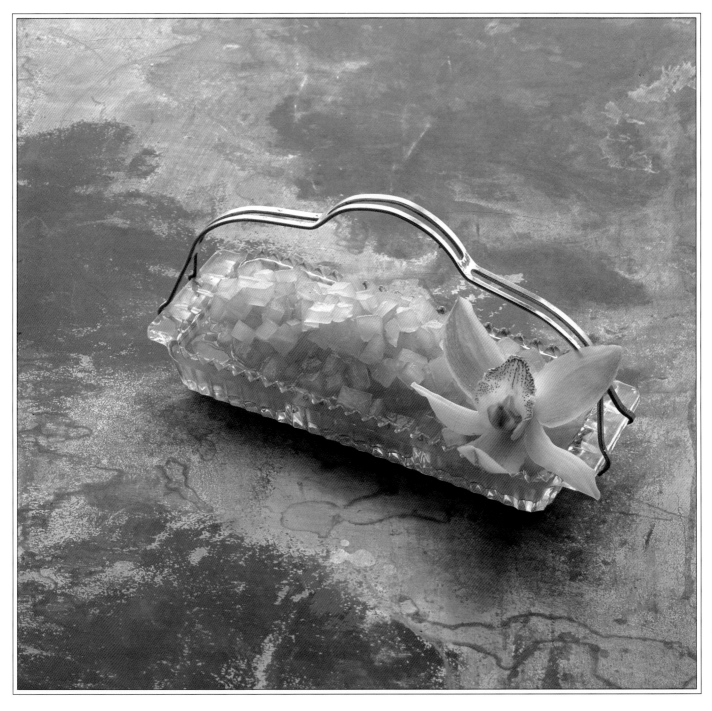

pickled watermelon rind.

Rind from 1 large watermelon
1/2 cup salt
2 1/2 cups cider vinegar
2 cups sugar
2 teaspoons cloves
1 small stick cinammon, in pieces
2 tablespoons whole allspice

Remove the pink pulp from the watermelon and cut the rind into pieces of the desired shape and size. Cover with boiling water and boil for 5 minutes. Drain and cool. Cut off the outer skin of the watermelon rind and remove any remaining bits of pink pulp. You should have about 8 cups of rind. Mix the salt with 3 cups of cold water and pour over the rind. Leave at room temperature for 6 hours. Drain, soak in several changes of fresh, cold water and drain again, then boil in fresh water until tender when pierced with a fork. Mix the vinegar, 1 cup of water and the sugar in a pot, then add the spices tied in a cheesecloth bag. Simmer until the sugar dissolves, then add the watermelon rind and simmer again until the rind is clear. Remove the spice bag and pack in sterilized jars (p. 168-9).

sunshine pie.

serves 8

dough.

1 1/4 cups sifted flour
1/2 teaspoon salt
1/2 cup butter or frozen margarine
3 tablespoons ice water

Mix the salt with the flour. Spread the butter over the flour and blend with a pair of knives until it looks sandy. Spoon the water in and mix with a fork. With your hands, make a ball of the dough, sprinkle flour on a flat surface and flatten it with a rolling pin. Prepare a pan by coating it lightly with butter and sprinkling it with flour. Cut a round piece of dough the size of the pan (including the sides) and press the dough into the pan, cutting off any overlaps. Puncture the dough with a fork and place the pan in a preheated oven at 350° until it begins to turn golden.
Fill the pan with custard (p. 69) and then decorate with the papaya.

Because of its fine texture and delicate flavor, this candied fruit is known as "peach impostor" it can be used in any recipe that calls for canned or conserved peaches.

papaya slices in syrup.

l small green papaya
1 lb. sugar
2 tablespoons white vinegar
1 cup maracuyá juice (p. 72)

Peel and finely slice papaya. Cook the papaya slices for 10 minutes in a pressure cooker with the sugar, maracuyá juice and vinegar. Remove, drain and cool.

melon with port.

serves 2

2 melons of different varieties
1 small cup port
Honey to taste

Slice one of the melons in half, remove the seeds and use it as a bowl. Spoon out the second melon's pulp in small balls and use these to fill the melon halves. Mix the port with the honey and spoon over the melon. Chill before serving.

pineapple in syrup.

2 cups chopped pineapple
1 cup sugar

Cook the pineapple with the sugar over medium heat, removing when the desired consistency has been obtained. For a light flavor, cook only until the fruit glistens. If you are looking for a syrupy taste, cook longer.

cabbage and pineapple salad.

serves 12

1 large pineapple cooked in
light syrup (p. 80) , chopped
and drained
2 cups cabbage, finely
chopped
8 envelopes pineapple gelatine
2 envelopes unflavored
gelatine
2 1/2 cups cream

Dissolve the pineapple
gelatine in 2 cups of boiling
water and the unflavored
gelatine in 1 cup of cold
water. Add this to the
pineapple and cabbage, mix
and leave for 15 minutes.
Then add the cream, mixing
well. Pour the salad into a
moistened pan and
refrigerate. After it has set,
remove and garnish the salad
before serving.

a papaya basket.

The shapes of fruits inspire us to use their shells as naturally appealing recipients for serving fruit. When you intend to use a fruit in this manner, look for a healthy one with good coloring. It shouldn't be too ripe. Fill it with its own pulp or with a variety of other fruits cut into different shapes and sizes. A sauce, a juice or a sprinkling of a suitable liqueur will also enhance your offering.

The Passifloraceae family is comprised of 12 genus and nearly 500 species some edible, others decorative. All passionflowers have a typical blossom conformation as their common denominator.

Their name comes from the shape of the flower, for the symbols of the passion of Jesus Christ can be discerned there: the nails are symbolized by the three stigmas, the crown of thorns by the many filiform petals, the chalice by the pedunculate ovary, the five wounds by other stamen and the lance by the leaves. All passionflowers contain passiflorin, a tranquilizing substance. For hyperactive children, a glass of passionfruit juice can work wonders at the end of the day to calm them.

Tree fern forest in Santa Rosa de Cabal, Risaralda.

Maracuyá

Passiflora edulis Sims.

The maracuyá is thought to have originated in Brazil.

Two types are known: the yellow maracuyá and the red variety. Within these, a great variety of colors, sizes and shapes can be found. The red maracuyá has been commercially cultivated in Kenya, South Africa and Australia.

The yellow variety thrives in tropical climates from 1,000 to 3,000 ft. above sea level. Additionally, it is the most resistant to diseases, the most productive, provides better fruit, has more juice and the tartest taste.

The maracuyá loses considerable weight shortly after being picked and its skin becomes wrinkled, but this does not affect the quality of the fruit. When it is ripe it simply falls to the ground; that is why it is said that this fruit is not picked but rather picked up. The main harvests are in January, May, June and July.

Although the ripe fruit is fairly sweet and refreshing, the maracuyá is usually thought to be too sour to eat fresh. It makes a wonderful, aromatic juice and is ideal for mixing with other fruit juices to help bring out their flavor and aroma. It is quite a special fruit and almost as versatile as lime for enhancing the flavors of other foods.

When selecting a maracuyá, campare the weight if the fruit to its size without worrying about the wrinkled skin; in fact, this indicates that the fruit is ripe.

Store in a cool place or in the refrigerator.

100 g. of edible fruit contain:	
Water	85.0 g.
Protein	0.8 g.
Fat	0.6 g.
Carbohydrates	2.4 g.
Fiber	0.2 g.
Ash	0 g.
Calcium	5.0 mg.
Phosphorus	18.0 mg.
Iron	0.3 mg.
Vitamin A	684 I.U.
Thiamine	0 mg.
Riboflavin	0.1 mg.
Niacin	2.24 mg.
Ascorbic Acid	20 mg.
Calories	50 cal.

Granadilla

Passiflora liguralis Jussieu.

The granadilla, a second type of passionfruit, is round and about 3 1/2 inches in diameter. Its shell is hard, which has the virtue of making transportation easier. It is cultivated in lands located between 4,000 and 7,000 ft. above sea level.

The delicately-flavored granadilla is considered perfect for babies as their first fruit. It is delicious at any time and mixes wonderfully with watermelon, papaya and melon, adding a dash of tartness to them.

Its shell should be yellow-orange in color and the freckled ones are of the best quality. It should be whole, smooth and shiny with no holes due to disease or insects. It is important to compare the size of the fruit to its weight because large, light fruits probably have little pulp inside. Granadillas should be stored in a cool, well-ventilated place. They keep well.

100 g. of edible fruit contain:	
Water	86.0 g.
Protein	1.1 g.
Fat	0.1 g.
Carbohydrate	11.6 g.
Fiber	0.3 g.
Ash	0.9 g.
Calcium	7 mg.
Phosphorus	30 mg.
Iron	0.8 mg.
Vitamin	0 I.U.
Thiamine	0 mg.
Riboflavin	0.10 mg.
Niacin	2.1 mg.
Ascorbic Acid	20 mg.
Calories	46 cal.

Curuba

Passiflora mollisima (H.B.K.) Bailey.

$\mathcal{T}$he curuba or mollifruit is elliptical in shape and measures approximately 3 inches in length. Its skin ranges from yellow-green to pale orange and is covered with a fine fuzz. Castillian curuba grows naturally between 5,500 and 8,000 ft. above sea level.

Two varieties are grown comercially. One wild strain, pale yellow, stumpy and thick and of quite irregular size, thrives only in the highlands and is definitely the best quality. The other has a longer shape, its color is a little more orange-like and its flavor is not quite as enticing.

The curuba is perhaps the most delicious fruit on earth for sherbets. When mixed with milk, cream or yogurt and a little sugar, and iced, it is incomparable. curuba also makes an exquisite mousse and ice cream.

Its juice has a low pH (3.4), while sugar levels barely reach 6%.

It is rich in ascorbic acid, phosphorus and vitamin A.

The fruit should have no signs of insect bites or bruises and it should be slightly soft to the touch. It should be stored in a cool place or in the refrigerator.

100 g. of edible fruit contain:	
Water	92.0 g.
Protein	0.6 g.
Fat	0.1 g.
Carbohydrates	6.3 g.
Fiber	0.3 g.
Ash	0.7 g.
Calcium	4 mg.
Phosphorus	20 mg.
Iron	0.4 mg.
Vitamin A	1,700 I.U.
Thiamine	0 mg.
Riboflavin	0.03 mg.
Niacin	2.5 mg.
Ascorbic Acid	70 mg.
Calories	25 cal.

Badea melon

Passiflora liguralis Jussieu.

$\mathcal{T}$he fruit is gourd-like and shaped like an elongated oval. It is large, measuring 9 to 14 inches in length and 4 1/2 and 7 inches in diameter. A badea can weigh over 3 lbs. and has a smooth, shiny surface ranging in color from almost white to pale yellow to yellow green. When ripe, sometimes its smooth milky and truly succulent pulp turns a bit pink, in a cavity full of numerous seeds surrounded by translucent and juicy arils.

It grows in humid lowlands from sea level to an altitude of 3,800 ft. above sea level.

Two varieties are easily distinguishable in Colombia: the Chocó and the Giant.

The badea is not very well known outside its own region, but it makes one of the most delicious and light fruit juices. To prepare badea juice, remove the pulp and add a small amount of sugar (not too much or the delicate flavor of the fruit will be overpowered). Mash this with a fork and then place it in the refrigerator for approximately one hour with a few ice cubes so that it can release its juices. Remove the pulp from the refrigerator, add the desired amount of water and strain. It is a delicately flavored fruit so the juice should be made rather concentrated; i.e. with little water.

To make a mousse, dice or blend the pulp briefly then strain it. Before blending badea pulp with other ingredients, make certain that all the seeds have been removed.

When selectng a badea. the proper color to look for is yellow or pale green, firm but not hard. If the exterior is a little pitted from insects, that does not affect the quality of the pulp.

It should be stored in a fresh, airy place.

100 g. of edible fruit contain:	
Water	87.9 g.
Protein	0.9 g.
Fat	0.2 g.
Carbohydrates	10.1 g.
Fiber	0.0 g.
Ash	0.9 g.
Calcium	10 mg.
Phosphorus	22 mg.
Iron	0.6 mg.
Vitamin A	70 I.U.
Thiamine	0 mg.
Riboflavin	0.11 mg.
Niacin	2.7 mg.
Ascorbic Acid	20 mg.
Calories	41 cal.

red snapper with maracuyá sauce and rosemary.

6 small red snappers
1/2 cup concentrated
maracuyá juice
White pepper, freshly ground
1/2 cup dry white wine
1/4 cup white vinegar
Grated peel of 1 orange
3 teaspoons spring onions,
finely chopped
1 teaspoon freshly ground
rosemary
2 tablespoons butter

In a small casserole, combine
the maracuyá juice, wine,
vinegar, orange peel and
rosemary. Simmer until this
sauce reduces by half. Season
the fish with salt and pepper
and fry them in butter until
golden. Pour the sauce over
the fish and serve.

beef loin with badea melon sauce.

serves 6

1 loin of beef
1 small badea melon
6 tablespoons butter
2 tablespoons oil
2 tablespoons grated onion
2 tablespoons Worcestershire
sauce
1 cup cream
Salt and pepper to taste
Laurel, thyme and oregano
Chopped parsley

First marinate the beef in the spices and the onion. Tie the meat and lightly brush it with oil to seal it, then brown it on all sides in very hot oil and butter. Place it in an ovenproof dish. Remove the seeds from the badea pulp, shred it by hand and mix it with the cream. Pour this sauce over the meat and place the dish in the oven at 400° for 20 minutes to obtain rare meat, or slightly longer

for medium or well-done. Before serving, garnish with finely chopped parsley.

curuba and guanábana meringue.

serves 12

8 egg whites
24 tablespoons sugar
(3 tablespoons for each egg
white)
1/2 teaspoon baking soda
1 ripe, medium-sized peeled
and pitted guanábana
8 curubas
1 cup cream
Sugar to taste
1 tablespoon brandy
3 tablespoons freshly grated
coconut, lightly browned in
the oven

Meringue
Beat the egg whites until stiff
and then slowly add the
sugar and baking soda.
Spread this evenly in 2
rectangular baking pans that
have been lined with oiled
waxed paper and place these
in the oven at 200° for 1 hour.

Sauce
Mix the cream with sugar
and brandy and divide in two.
Mix one part with the
guanábana and the other
with the curuba. Place one
meringue on a dish and cover
with the guanábana sauce.
Then place the other
meringue top of the first and
cover it with the curuba
sauce. Top with the grated
coconut.

The tart flavor of the curuba
gives this pastry a special
touch.

curuba mousse.

2 cups curuba juice
6 egg whites beaten until stiff
1 1/2 cups sugar
2 1/2 tablespoons unflavored gelatine

Soak the gelatine in 1/4 cup of cold water. On a hot stove, bring the fruit juice and the sugar to boiling point and then add the gelatine. When this liquid becomes smooth, allow to cool and freeze. Before it has fully set, remove from the freezer and blend until frothy. Fold in the egg whites and pour the mixture into a pan which has been lightly coated with sweet almond oil. Keep in the refrigerator until it sets fully.

After removing the mousse from the pan, place it in a serving dish and cover it with the following sauce:

curuba sauce.

2 tablespoons cornstarch
1 cup milk
1 1/2 cups curuba juice
Sugar to taste
1 or 2 tablespoons cream, optional

Dissolve cornstarch in the milk, add sugar to taste and simmer until obtaining heavy syrup (p. 80). Allow to cool. Mix in the curuba juice, stirring until the syrup is smooth. This sauce can also be made with blackberries or oranges.

maracuyá ice cream in the shell.

serves 12

1 cup concentrated maracuyá juice (p. 72)
1 can condensed milk
2 1/2 cups cream
2 egg whites beaten until stiff
Grated peel of 1 lime

Carefully slice the maracuyás in half, remove the pulp and set aside the shells. Blend the juice with the remaining ingredients, then place this in a container and leave it in the freezer until it begins to set. Remove, blend again and lightly fold in the egg whites. Fill the fruit shells with this mixture and put them in the freezer. Remove 10 minutes before serving. Garnish with half an uchuva and a sprig of mint.

maracuyá and pineapple mousse.

serves 8

1/2 glass concentrated
maracuyá juice (p. 72)
1 pineapple in light syrup
(p. 54), chopped and drained
1 can condensed milk
1 cup cream
3 envelopes unsweetened
gelatine
1/4 cup warm water
4 egg whites beaten until stiff
Juice of 1 lime

Lightly blend the pineapple
with the maracuyá juice,
leaving shreds of pineapple.
Place this in a pot, add the
lime juice and bring it to a
boil. Add the gelatine,
previously dissolved in 1/4
cup of cold water. Then add
the condensed milk and
cream. Now fold in the egg
whites, using a wooden
spoon, and spread the mix
evenly in a lightly oiled pan.
Leave the mousse in the
refrigerator for 2 hours or
until it sets. Place on a dish

and cover with the following
sauce:

custard.

2 cups milk
3 egg yolks
1 tablespoon cornflour
1/2 cup sugar
Grated peel of 1 lime
1 tablespoon brandy or rum
1 tablespoon butter
1 1/2 cups cream

Beat the yolks with the sugar
and flour. Heat the milk, add
the yolks and stir with a
wooden spoon without
allowing the milk to boil,
adding the lime and the
brandy and letting the sauce
thicken. Allow to cool and
add the cream.

granadilla juice.

Break open the fruits and
place the pulp in a strainer
and press it with a wooden
spoon until only the seeds
remain. This juice does not
need to be sweetened.

Granadilla juice is
recommended for babies as
their first fruit juice.

maracuyá cocktails.

serves 6

*2 cups concentrated
maracuyá juice
3 small cups aguardiente (or
anisette cordial)
Sugar to taste
1/4 glass club soda
4 ice cubes*

Blend the ingredients, then
serve in small cups on
crushed ice. Garnish with a
sprig of mint. Aguardiente is
a strong Colombian spirit
with an anise flavor. If you
use anisette cordial instead,
reduce the amount of sugar.

Here's another delicious
maracuyá cocktail:

*2 cups concentrated
maracuyá juice (p. 72)
1 bottle iced white wine
Sugar to taste*

Sweeten the juice, add the
wine and serve in glasses.

concentrated curuba or maracuyá juice.

12 curubas or maracuyás
1/4 cup sugar

To prepare a good concentrated curuba or maracuyá juice you must prevent the seeds from breaking because they will give the juice a bitter taste.
Open each fruit and extract the pulp, placing it in a nonmetallic container. Mix in the sugar and press with a fork, then leave for 15 minutes. Blend at very low speed and then strain.
To make a delicious crème, use 1 cup of concentrated juice for every 3 cups of cold milk, blending at high speed.
Crèmes can be served with vanilla ice cream or whipped cream.

Citrus fruits and their like come from southeastern Asia and India, where they thrive in the wild. Thousands of years ago, at the time of the development of agriculture, hybrids were created by crossbreeding different citrus species. They were first introduced to the Mediterranean at the beginning of the 16th century and then later spread to all of Europe. From there the Spaniards and the Portuguese brought them to the New World where they adapted splendidly, aided by the climate and by soil conditions.

Citrus types include a great variety of fruits such as oranges, mandarin oranges, lemons, limes and grapefruits. In Colombia, they can be found growing from sea level up to 5700 ft.

Colombian citrus varieties come from seeds that were brought by the Europeans and from grafted species. They are outstanding for their size, fragrance, color, juice content, flavor and for the consistency of their rind.

In general, citrus fruit is consumed and appreciated all over the world for its well-known vitamin content, especially vitamin C.

Stands of bamboo and carboneros in Manizales, Caldas.

Orange

Citrus aurantium L.

The common or Creole orange includes almost one hundred varieties, many of which have resulted from crossbreeding. The tasty and popular Valencia orange is the best known of the eating oranges. They are ideal for preparing juice but they are also very good peeled and eaten fresh. Among the navel oranges, the Washington variety enjoys great popularity due to its uniform quality, size, appearance and taste. Navel oranges are only used only for eating because they contain limein, a somewhat bitter substance which precludes their use in juice or concentrates. Other well-known varieties are the Lerma, Salerma, Hamlin and Ruby oranges. Among the bitter oranges, there are the common bitter orange, other hybrids and the Taiwan variety. Bitter oranges are not in great demand and they are grown principally for crossbreeding.

A fresh orange, freshly sectioned, in addition to providing juice also contains fiber, an important aid to digestion, also cleansing the organism. The orange is one of the most highly appreciated and healthy fruits, appreciated for its tonic and purifying tributes.

The orange is a most versatile ingredient in the kitchen. It provides a bite to fruit salads, makes perhaps the best marmalade of any fruit Orange marmalade, with its characteristic and inimitable bittersweet flavor, is one of the delights of breakfast. And chocolate-covered candied orange rind is a true delicacy.

Orange juice at the beginning of the day provides pure liquid energy, with a sweetness that puts one's disposition on track and an acid twist rather conducive to paying attention. It is no accident that millions of people all over the world make the daily transition from sleep to activity by drinking a glass of fresh orange juice.

Oranges should be firm to the touch and free of any blemishes or bruises. The rind of several oranges that are good for juice can be green.

Oranges keep well in a fresh place, but it is advisable to store them in the refrigerator or to freeze the pulp or freshly-squeezed juice.

100 g. of edible fruit contain:	
Water	89.0 g.
Protein	0.7 g.
Fat	0.1 g.
Carbohydrates	9.0 g.
Fiber	0.7 g.
Ash	0.5 g.
Calcium	19 mg.
Phosphorus	22 mg.
Iron	0.4 mg.
Vitamin A	0 I.U.
Thiamine	0.08 mg.
Riboflavin	0.03 mg.
Niacin	0.3 mg.
Ascorbic Acid	60 mg.
Calories	35 cal.

Grapefruit

Citrus paradisii Macfadyen.

The grapefruit, a thin-skinned, yellow fruit, has a pleasant although occasionally bitter flavor. Besides its peculiar, tangy sweetness, the grapefruit has diverse nutritional and curative properties. To produce a large fruit, the climate must be hotter than is required for the mandarin or common orange. For this reason, they are usually cultivated in the hottest areas.

The "Ruby Red" variety has an exceptionally sweet and deep-colored pulp. It is usually eaten as part of a meal, espécially in low fat diets. The "Marsh" variety is very popular among growers, not only because it was the first seedless variety but also because it has been very receptive to crossbreeding and creating other pink varieties.

100 g. of edible fruit contain:	
Water	90.3 g.
Protein	0.7 g.
Fat	0.1 g.
Carbohydrates	7.5 g.
Fiber	0.9 g.
Ash	0.5 g.
Calcium	27 mg.
Phosphoru	32 mg.
Iron	0.5 mg.
Vitamin A	0 I.U.
Thiamine	0.06 mg.
Riboflavin	0.02 mg.
Niacin	0.2 mg.
Ascorbic Acid	40 mg.
Calories	30 cal.

Mandarin orange

Citrus reticulata Blanco.

Among citrus fruits, the small and flattened orange known as the mandarin, or tangerine, is considered a delicacy because of its optimum quality and distinctive sweet flavor.

There are a multitude of varieties, from the tiny compact ones to the large mandarins whose rind loosely adheres to the fruit.

The colors of the peel range from deep green to orange and also pale yellow. All of the different varieties are delicious.

The mandarin is truly a noble fruit. When in season, it is a very inexpensive source of vitamin C. Its juice is very good for starting babies on citrus fruits and it is delicious substitute for orange juice.

Because it is easy to peel and section by hand, the mandarin is convenient for lunch boxes and picnics.

It should be firm to the touch when gently squeezed. There should be no marks or spots from disease or insects and it should give off a pleasant fragrance.

It is a fruit that keeps well, easily stored in a fresh place or the refrigerator.

Outstanding hybrids are the Oneco and Tangelo oranges. This latter is a hybrid produced from crossbreeding the mandarin orange and the grapefruit, providing a particularly juicy, sweet and high-quality fruit. The Oneco is the most tropical variety.

100 g. of part fruit contain:	
Water	88.8 g.
Protein	0.7 g.
Fat	0.1 g.
Carbohydrates	9.5 g.
Fiber	0.5 g.
Ash	0.4 g.
Calcium	24 mg.
Phosphorus	19 mg.
Iron	0.2 mg.
Vitamin A	1000 I.U.
Thiamine	0.11 mg.
Riboflavin	0.03 mg.
Niacin	0.3 mg.
Ascorbic Acid	24 mg.
Calories	38 cal.

Lime

Citrus aurantifolia (Chr.) Swingle.

The lime distinguishes itself from other citrus fruits because of its size. color and flavor. It is commonly used because of its multiple properties. The best known varieties are the common or Castillian lime and the Tahiti lime. The former is quite small, with a shiny green rind; it can be found growing in the wild. A second variety, also known as the Persian lime, is juicier, larger and has a darker green rind, more textured and slightly thicker. There are also other varieties of limes such as the Mandarin Lime, which has a slightly sweet flavor and tangerine-colored pulp and the large, wrinkled variety which is particularly sour, good primarily for crossbreeding.

The lime is one of the most widely-used medicinal products to come from the Plant Kingdom.

Indeed, it has been said of the lime that it is the panacea which God put within our reach to cure all diseases and that it is humanity's grand laboratory or pharmacy.

Despite its acidity, it is a powerful neutralizer for the acid levels in the blood. Lime is also in common use as a purifying agent. It has excellent disinfectant properties and its rind contains essential oils.

Especially in the tropics, lime is used for almost everything. Lime for diarrhea, lime for the gums, lime for colds, lime for sustaining health and vigor. One must take care to not exagerate its remedial properties, but in fact, they are extensive.

In the kitchen, lime juice is the best substitute for and a good complement to vinegar, as well as being a widely used ingredient in its own right. It makes a tangy drink, helps other fruits retain their color, and enhances their flavor.

Select limes that appear full, are not yellowed or wrinkled and smell fresh.

Store them in a cool place or in the refrigerator. To get the most from the fruit when squeezing for juice, warm the lime first, for this dilates the membranes and releases more juice.

100 g. edible fruit contain:	
Water	91.8 g.
Protein	0.3 g.
Fat	0.3 g.
Carbohydrates	6.3 g.
Fiber	1.0 g.
Ash	0.3 g.
Calcium	13 mg.
Phosphorus	14 mg.
Iron	0.4 mg.
Vitamin A	0 I.U.
Thiamine	0.02 mg.
Riboflavin	0.02 mg.
Niacin	0.1 mg.
Ascorbic Acid	25 mg.
Calories	26 cal.

small orange rolls.

6 oranges
A pinch of baking soda
2 lbs. sugar

Wash the oranges and slice them into thick wheels, leaving the peel but removing the seeds. In a pot, cover the orange slices with water, add the bicarbonate and cook until tender. Drain and cut into strips. Roll these pieces up and fasten them with a wooden toothpick. Cook in water and sugar until the consistency of light syrup is obtained. The fruit should glisten at this point.

syrups.

Many fruits can be cooked in sugar and water. A few drops of lime juice enliven the taste of the syrups made in this manner. Glucose may be added to prevent crystallization. The consistency of syrups varies:

light
Dissolve 1/2 cup of sugar in 1 cup of water and cook over moderate heat. When the syrup falls from a spoon in a continuous line, you have light syrup.

medium
Dissolve 1 cup of sugar in 1 cup of water and cook over moderate heat. When the syrup falls from a spoon as a ribbon, you have medium syrup.

heavy
Dissolve 1 1/2 cups of sugar in 1 cup of water and cook over moderate heat. When a drop of the syrup placed in cold water can be shaped into a ball with your fingers, you have heavy syrup.

caramel
Use the same proportion of sugar and water as for heavy syrup. Cook until a drop of syrup placed in cold water becomes a crystallized line.

lime peel halves in syrup.

20 large green limes
1 1/2 lbs. sugar
A pinch of bicarbonate

Grate the limes very lightly and wash them to take the edge off their bitter taste. Slice each fruit in half and remove all of the pulp. In a pan, cover the limes with water, add a pinch of bicarbonate and boil for 15 minutes. Drain and place in 1 quart of water with the sugar. Simmer until the fruit shells look glazed.

candied citrus peel.

2 grapefruits, oranges or limes
2 cups sugar
A pinch of bicarbonate

Peel the fruit into large strips, cover them with cold water and soak for 30 minutes, then drain. In a pan, cover the peel with water, add the bicarbonate and simmer until soft. Cut the peel into small strips. Over low heat, dissolve 1 1/2 lbs. of sugar in 1 1/4 cups of water, add the peel and simmer for 1 hour. Cover and leave overnight. Then heat the peel until the syrup reaches boiling point, allow to cool and drain. Sprinkle the pieces of peel with sugar, dry them on paper and then store in jars. They should remain fresh for months. If not, put a lemon in the container for a day or two.

grapefruit with honey.

serves 2

1 grapefruit
Honey
2 tablespoons sherry
1 cherry

Slice the grapefruit in half, extract the pulp, remove the pits and trim the white peel. Mix the pulp with the honey and sherry. Fill the shells with this and place them in the oven at 350°. Garnish with the cherry. You can use different varieties of grapefruit.

grapefruit in special cream.

serves 1

5 sections of grapefruit
3 tablespoons of homemade
mayonnaise
1 tablespoon cream
2 tablespoons avocado purée

Peel the grapefruit, separate
5 sections and peel each one
of these. Use a fork to mix
the other ingredients. Spread
this sauce on the plate and
place the grapefruit sections
on it.

homemade mayonnaise.

1 egg
1 teaspoon salt
1 teaspoon sugar
1 teaspoon mustard
1 teaspoon vinegar
Pepper to taste
A few drops lime juice
1/4 cup parsley
1 cup salad oil

Set the oil aside and blend
the remaining ingredients.
When the mix is smooth, set
the blender at low speed and
add the oil in a fine trickle.

lime parfait.

5 egg whites
1 1/2 cups sugar
1/2 cup lime juice
Grated peel of 1 lime
3 envelopes unflavored
gelatine
1/2 cup water

Soak the gelatine in 1/4 cup of cold water and then dissolve it in 1/4 cup of very hot water. Beat the egg whites until stiff. Continue to beat and slowly add the sugar, lime juice and lime peel. Mix in the gelatine. Place in the refrigerator. When the mixture begins to set, remove from the refrigerator, blend and then spread evenly in a lightly oiled pan. Leave until it sets.

orange cake.

1 lb. butter
1 lb. sugar
3 teaspoons salt
Grated peel of two oranges
1 cup orange juice
1 cup sugar
8 eggs
1 lb. flour (sift three times)
4 teaspoons baking powder
4 teaspoons lime juice

Beat the butter, salt and grated orange peel thoroughly. Add the sugar, then add the eggs one by one, beating slowly. Sift the dry ingredients and add them to the batter, alternating with the juices. Mix well, then spread evenly in a mold which has been greased and sprinkled with flour. Bake in a pre-heated oven at 350° for 1 hour. After the cake has cooled, cover with orange icing.

orange icing.

1 lb. powdered sugar
1 envelope unsweetened gelatine
1 tablespoon glucose
1 tablespoon glicerine
1/4 cup orange juice
Yellow coloring

Dissolve the gelatine in warmed orange juice. Over low heat, add the glucose and the glicerine. Stir until syrupy but do not allow to boil. On a table, spread the sugar, placing an egg in the middle. Add the syrup slowly, stirring with a knife. Then knead thoroughly until the paste is smooth and does not stick. With a rolling pin, spread evenly in a circle the size of the cake. Moisten the cake and place the icing on it.

mandarin orange rice.

serves 6

2 cups rice
2 cups juice
2 cups water
2 tablespoons butter
1 tablespoon oil
1 teaspoon salt
1 teaspoon sugar
1 orange peel cut into thin strips
1/2 teaspoon baking soda

Place the peel in very hot water with baking soda for 5 minutes, then drain. Fry the rice lightly in the butter and oil for 3 minutes, stirring constantly. To the rice, add the water, orange juice, salt and sugar. Boil over medium heat until the liquid has completely evaporated, then cover tightly and leave over very low heat for a further 40 minutes.

Remove from heat, mix in part of the orange peels, place on a dish and garnish with the remaining peels.

quail in orange sauce.

serves 4

12 quails
1 leaf laurel
1 small white onion
1/2 tablespoon thyme
1 cup port
1 tablespoon Worcestershire
sauce
Juice of 2 oranges
1 tablespoon cooking oil
Salt and pepper to taste

In a large receptacle, mix all the ingredients and leave the birds to marinate for 1 hour. Then add 2 cups of water and simmer until tender.

orange sauce.

6 oranges
1/2 cup sugar
1 tablespoon butter
1 cup port
2 tablespoons cornstarch

Make juice from the oranges. Trim some of the peel and slice it into thin strips, placing them briefly in boiling water three times to remove their bitter taste.

Put the sugar in a saucepan and heat it until it turns caramel color, then add the orange juice. Separately, dissolve the cornstarch and gradually add it to the simmering juice, stirring constantly for 10 minutes to prevent sticking. Then add the butter, port and blanched peel. This sauce is good for many other dishes.

oranges and cohune nuts in aguardiente.

5 oranges
A handful of cohune nuts
1 bottle aguardiente
1/2 bottle rum
2 lbs. sugar dissolved in 2
cups water
5 cloves
2 tablespoons vanilla

Choose juicy and ripe oranges with fine-looking peel. Peel them and trim off all the white bits. Puncture the fruit repeatedly with a fork or a pin. Cut it into sections and remove all the seeds. In a recipient, mix all the ingredients except the orange pieces and the nuts, then add these, making sure they are totally covered by the liquid. Cover and leave in a dark place. The fruit can be eaten after 3 days. Serve alone, on ice cream or with Chantilly cream.

four lemonades.

light.

Peel of three limes
1 quart fresh water
3 cups sugar
Juice of 3 limes

Boil the water and leave the peel in it for 3 minutes. Strain and add the sugar and the lime juice, then bring to a boil to dissolve the sugar. Allow to cool and place in the refrigerator.

rose.

Rose petals
1 quart fresh water
Sugar to taste
Juice of 3 limes

Place a handful of rose petals in the bottom of a recipient and pour 1 quart of boiling water over them, leave for 1 hour to macerate. Strain, then add the lime juice and sugar.

with peel.

2 limes
1 quart fresh water
Sugar to taste
3 ice cubes

Cut off the tops and bottoms of the limes, then slice them and remove the seeds. Blend the fruit with the water, sugar and ice.

crème.

1 bottle of ice cold milk
Sugar to taste
1/2 cup of lime juice
Grated peel of 1 lime

Blend the milk with the sugar, then add the lime juice and blend again. Serve in cups over crushed ice and garnish with grated lime peel.

iced mandarin oranges in the shell

6 tangerines with stems
and leaves if possible
1/2 can condensed milk
2 egg whites beaten until stiff
Grated peel of 1 tangerine
1 cup cream

Cut off the tops of the tangerines. Carefully remove all the pulp, pit them and make a concentrated juice. Blend in the condensed milk and the cream and leave in the refrigerator for 2 hours, after which blend again and gently fold in the egg whites with a wooden spoon. Fill the shells, cover them with their own tops and freeze. Remove 10 minutes before serving. The iced fruit can be served with appropriate biscuits. Sprinkle grated peel over the fruit before serving.

Mist forest and sietecueros in the Páramo de Letras, Tolima.

Early fig

Ficus carica L.

Figs came from Syria and their cultivation later spread to China and India. But etchings of figs were also found on the Geza Pyramid, Aristotle mentioned the antiquity of their cultivation and Roman poets made several references to figs at different times. This is thus a characteristic and well-beloved fruit of early cultures.

Figs have been cultivated all around the Mediterranean since ancient times. The Spaniards brought them to America, and since the Colonial period they have graced orchards and gardens in medium to cold climates. It is one of the most ancient fruit-bearing trees. In paintings, the fig tree, replete with fruit, symbolized abundance and peace. During the Middle Ages, figs and fig leaves were believed to have magical and medicinal properties. Shredded fig leaves mixed with tobacco make a pipe tobacco that many people find delightful.

More than 700 varieties of fig trees exist worldwide, all of which originated in the Ficus carica species and the sativa subspecies, known as the domestic fig.

The fig in its first stage, the early fig, is a small green fruit that is used to make preserves, marmalades and fillings for pastries. It is a nutritious food that helps ward off fatigue. The ripe fig, on the other hand, is harvested in the Autumn in countries with seasons.

Early figs cooked in syrup, with just a spoonful of arequipe, a wonderful concoction of sugar and milk, and a slice of fresh farmer's cheese, or any combination of two of the latter three elements, is high on the list of "combined" or "married" desserts in the cuisine of the Colombian Andes. Ask for "dulce de brevas con arequipe y queso". It is a taste acquired in youth that lasts a lifetime.

Early figs are usually picked green. They should be free of blemishes and spots from insects and firm when gently squeezed. If, on the other hand, ripe figs are what you want, look for a darker-colored fruit, between green and dark purple. This fig should be soft and, when opened, pink inside; it can be eaten skin and all.

Ideally, figs should be used as soon after being picked as possible. If that is not feasible, they can be stored for a short time in a cool place.

100 g. of edible fruit contain:	
Water	86.1 g.
Protein	1.7 g.
Fat	0.3 g.
Carbohydrate s	8.6 g.
Fiber	2.5 g.
Ash	0.8 g.
Calcium	68 mg.
Phosphorus	34 mg.
Iron	0.5 mg.
Vitamin A	20 I.U.
Thiamine	0.05 mg.
Riboflavin	0.06 mg.
Niacin	0.3 mg.
Ascorbic Acid	18 mg.
Calories	39 cal.

Blackberry

Rubus glaucus Bentham.

The best known species of the Rubus genus are American.

In Colombia, nine edible species and some 40 wild species have been identified. The Castillian blackberry, native to America, is the best known variety. Purple and attractive, with a sweet and sour taste before ripening, it turns dark and sweet when ripe and has a pleasant aroma. The plants themselves are thorny vines that make good fences and help to control erosion.

Blackberries are delicious off the vine, in jams and jellies, preserves, ice creams and tarts. Blackberry sauce is delectable with meats and poultry.

The color of the berry is an important factor; it should be a deep purple. One bad berry will spoil the rest. They should be used as soon as possible, but they can be stored in the refrigerator.

100 g. of edible fruit contain:	
Water	93.3 g.
Protein	0.6 g.
Fat	0.1 g.
Carbohydrates	5.6 g.
Fiber	0 g.
Ash	0.4 g.
Calcium	18 mg.
Phosphorus	14 mg.
Iron	1.2 mg.
Vitamin A	0.00 I.U.
Thiamine	0.02 mg.
Riboflavin	0.04 mg.
Niacin	0.4 mg.
Ascorbic Acid	15 mg.
Calories	23 cal.

Uchuva

Physalis peruviana L.

The uvilla or uchuva, sometimes known as the Cape gooseberry, comes from the South American Andes, where it grows freely in the colder lands.

There are 45 known varieties, all of which are wild.

It is an herbaceous plant, often thought to be a weed.

It has the advantage of being a wild undomesticated plant of hardy disposition, growing in all kinds of soil and tolerating highly variable amounts of sunshine. The plant also has a natural resistance to pests and disease.

At present, physalis is under cultivation due to its increasing popularity. This berry has attracted much attention because of its appearance, which complements salads and desserts. Thanks to its unusual flavor, physalis makes an original and pleasing marmalade.

It is generally sold as it comes from the bush, ensconced in its characteristic pod of dry leaves; indeed, few fruits come more conveniently packaged. The best physalis are the larger ones, firm and orange in color. The green ones are extremely bitter and once harvested they do not ripen.

100 g. of edible fruit contain:	
Water	85.9 g.
Protein	1.5 g.
Fat	0.5 g.
Carbohydrate	11.0 g.
Fiber	0.4 g.
Ash	0.7 g.
Calcium	9 mg.
Phosphorus	21 mg.
Iron	1.7 mg.
Vitamin A	1,730 I.U.
Thiamine	0.01 mg.
Riboflavin	0.17 mg.
Niacin	0.8 mg.
Ascorbic Acid	20 mg.
Calories	49 cal.

Tamarillo

Cyphomandra betacea (Cav.) Sendt.

Native to the Peruvian Andes and to certain regions of Ecuador, Bolivia and Chile, the tamarillo could perhaps have developed at the same time in the mountains of Java. In Colombia, this fruit thrives in areas from 3,000 to 8,000 ft. above sea level.

The tamarillo is an elliptically-shaped fruit that measures 3 to 5 inches in length and has a diameter of about 2 inches at its widest point. It is smooth and the skin is very bitter and inedible. It has seeds that are very similar to that of the tomato for which reason it is also know as the "tree tomato". The tamarillo is low in calories and rich in vitamin A. It is not a sweet fruit but it is widely used to make fruit juices and preserves. It also makes a delicious and unusual marmalade.

When ripe, the tamarillo takes on a bright orange color. Its skin is slick and shiny. The fruit should not be wrinkled, and it should be somewhat soft to the touch.

Tamarillos should be left at room temperature until they are fairly soft. When the right degree of ripeness has been reached, the fruit can be stored in the refrigerator.

100 g. of edible fruit contain:	
Water	89.7 g.
Protein	1.4 g.
Fat	0.1 g.
Carbohydrates	7.0 g.
Fiber	1.1 g.
Ash	0.7 g.
Calcium	6 mg.
Phosphorus	22 mg.
Iron	0.4 mg.
Vitamin A	1,000 I.U.
Thiamine	0.05 mg.
Riboflavin	0.03 mg.
Niacin	1.1 mg.
Ascorbic Acid	25 mg.
Calories	30 cal.

Tamarind

Tamarindus indica L.

We know that when the Arabs went to India, they gave the name of tamr-hindi to this luxuriant and benevolent shade and fruit tree with elegant yellow flowers.

The fruit is a small, elongated, thin-skinned gourd surrounding numerous seeds suspended in a pulp that is as sweet as it is sour. It is more refreshing and mild than citrus fruits and has an aroma and flavor that have no substitute in oriental cuisine. The tamarind has been widely adapted to the taste and customs of the Colombian coasts.

The tamarind is generally to be found as a paste and it can be eaten as a sweet, much like dates or raisins. To use the fruit, take the desired amount, mix it with water and blend with a hand beater or whisk. Strain the mixture to remove the seeds: what remains is a delicious, refreshing juice ready for drinking over ice or for use in preparing exotic sauces or fillings for pastries.

If the fruit is bought in its natural state, the gourd has to be opened by hand and the seeds and pulp extracted. The fruit should be stored in a cool place and the pulp preferably in the refrigerator.

100 g. of edible fruit contain:	
Water	18.4 g.
Protein	5.4 g.
Fat	0.5 g.
Carbohydrates	61.3 g.
Fiber	11.9 g.
Ash	2.5 g.
Calcium	81 mg.
Phosphorus	86 mg.
Iron	1.1 mg.
Vitamin	0 I.U.
Thiamine	0.20 mg.
Riboflavin	0.19 mg.
Niacin	2.5 mg.
Ascorbic Acid	18 mg.
Calories	280 cal.

Guava

Psidium guajaba L.

*T*he guava comes from the American tropics, where it still grows mostly in the wild. The Spaniards carried it across the Pacific to the Philippine Islands and the Portuguese planted it in their colonies in India. The guava later spread to all tropical regions.

There are some 150 varieties of this very basic fruit in the American tropical and subtropical regions, divided into pink pulp and white pulp groups. The different guavas can better be classified as types rather than varieties. Studies have allowed experts to recommend four types in particular: Extranjero, Polo nuevo, Red and D-14.

Generally, the guava varies from round to oval in shape, and is sometimes pear-shaped. Its weight varies from 1 oz. to close to 1 lb. The larger-sized guava, known as the sour guava (Psidium acutangulum), is very acid; it is one of the few tropical fruits that is eaten green. The skin of the sweet guava, when ripe, is usually yellow with white and pink shading. Its structure varies from those with very thin skins, a multitude of small seeds and salmon color, with firm pulp, to those with a thick shell and few seeds.

The sweet, juicy kind is eaten as fruit and both skin and pulp are used in the preparation of pastries.

Sour guava pulp is somewhat soft, pungent and quite delicious as a juice or an ice cream.

Although guavas can be eaten fresh, they is usually used processed. Guava paste, candy and jellies are made industrially.

This fruit's pulp provides the basis for a wine that has a good bouquet and also for a delicious liqueur - guava cream.

Guavas, in addition to containing a high percentage of carbohydrates, also have protein and are rich in vitamin C. They provide from two to five times more vitamin C than orange juice.

Dehydrated and powdered guava juice was used during the Second World War to fortify troop rations for the Allied forces. It has the advantage of being a highly digestible fruit. Production is more or less constant all year long.

Guavas should be of a good size, firm and with no marks from insects. If a fruit looks a little deteriorated on the outside, this will not affect its taste. Sour guavas are soft and yellow-green; if their skin is dark, this will not affect the fruit.

Guavas should be used or processed as soon as possible, for once picked the fruit decomposes rapidly. They can also be stored in the refrigerator.

100 g. of edible fruit contain:	Pink Pulp	White Pulp
Water	86.0	86.0 g.
Protein	0.9	0.9 g.
Fat	0.1	0.1 g.
Carbohydrates	9.5	9.5 g.
Fiber	2.8	2.8 g.
Ash	0.7	0.7 g.
Calcium	17	15 mg.
Phosphorus	30	22 mg.
Iron	0.7	0.6 mg.
Vitamin A	400	0 I.U.
Thiamine	0.05	0.03 mg.
Riboflavin	0.03	0.03 mg.
Niacin	0.6	0.6 mg.
Ascorbic Acid	200	240 mg.
Calories	36	36 cal.

guava jelly.

9 lbs. fresh, ripe guavas
1 1/2 lbs. sugar

Wash the guavas and break them up by hand, covering them with water in a bowl. Leave the fruit overnight hung in clean cheesecloth so all the liquid can drain off. On the following day, mix the liquid with the sugar and make a jelly over high heat. When this begins to jell, pour it into a moistened pan and leave it until it sets. Remove from pan and serve.

guava shells.

3 dozen guavas
2 lbs. sugar

Peel the outer skin off the guavas and cut them into halves. Spoon out the pulp. Making sure they are covered with water, simmer the shells until tender. Add the sugar and simmer again until the fruit glistens.

early figs in syrup.

serves 12

2 1/2 lbs. early figs
2 1/2 lbs. sugar or brown
sugar loaf
1 lime

Wash the figs and peel them finely with a potato parer to eliminate their bitter taste, then wash again. Cut them in four lengthwise, cover with water in a bowl and add the lime juice. Boil water in a pot, add the fig pieces and simmer until tender. Drain. Dissolve the sugar in water and simmer the figs in this for 6 hours, adding water or sugar if necessary.

Early figs are not difficult to prepare but the task is time consuming. Prepare a good sized batch and store in vacuum-packed jars (pp.168-9) they are the basis for dozens of pastries, cakes, fillings and so on.
They are an exquisite sweetmeat; served with arequipe and slice of fresh cheese, they are a delicacy.

uchuva marmalade with elderberry flowers.

1 lb. uchuvas
1 lb. brown sugar
1 cup water
Elderberry flowers

Wash the uchuvas. Make a syrup with the water and sugar and when it begins to thicken, add the fruit. Simmer for 15 minutes or until the marmalade has reached the desired consistency. Remove from heat and add the finely chopped elderberry flowers. Preserve in sterilized jars (p. 168-9).

sun-sweetened blackberries.

Blackberries marinated in aguardiente (p. 105)
1 lightly-beaten egg white
Granulated sugar

Put a toothpick though each berry and roll it in the egg white and then in the sugar. Fix the toothpicks on a grapefruit half and place it in the sun to dry.

blackberry aguardiente.

2 lbs. hulled ripe blackberries
2 bottles aguardiente

Place the berries in a glass or enameled container and marinate in the aguardiente for 2 months. Strain using a cheesecloth and keep in bottles. The blackberries which have lost their color can be sun-sweetened (see previous recipe).

blackberry ice cream.

serves 8

1 lb. washed and hulled
blackberries
1 1/2 cups sugar
1 cup cream
2 envelopes unsweetened
gelatine
1 tablespoon lime juice

Soak the gelatine in 1/2 cup
of cold water and then
dissolve it in 1/2 cup of very
hot water. Blend the berries
in 1 cup of water, then add
the sugar and the lime juice.
Strain the juice and mix it
with the gelatine. Freeze for
1 hour, then remove, blend
thoroughly with the cream
and refrigerate. This ice
cream can be served with
blackberries in syrup.

blackberries in syrup.

1 lb. washed and hulled
blackberries
1 lb. sugar
1 tablespoon lime juice

Place all the ingredients in a
heavy pot and simmer until
all the berries are covered in
froth. These berries can also
be served with a simple
cheese or unsalted fresh
cheese.

tamarillo mousse.

6 tamarillos
2 1/2 envelopes unflavored gelatine
4 egg whites beaten until stiff
1/2 cup cream

Dissolve the gelatine in 1/2 cup of water. Blend the peeled tamarillos with 1 1/2 cups of water and sugar to taste. Drain and place in a saucepan over medium heat until the juice comes to a boil. Remove from heat and slowly stir in the gelatine until the mix becomes smooth and then keep it in an enameled container in the freezer for 30 minutes or until it sets. Remove, add the cream and blend. Place this mix in the refrigerator for 20 minutes until it begins to set. Remove and blend again, then fold in the egg whites with a wooden spoon. Pour the mix into a lightly oiled or moistened mold and store in the refrigerator until the mousse sets. Before serving, remove from mold and cover with Chantilly cream (p. 108), special custard (p. 69) or a fruit sauce (pp. 67, 110).

uchuva mille feuilles.

serves 8

1/2 lb. pastry (p. 109)
1/2 lb. uchuvas
Grated peel of 2 limes
2 cups Chantilly cream

Boil water and dunk the uchuvas in it, then peel them and set them aside. Roll out the dough and cut out two 5 1/2 in. by 9 in. rectangles. Place one of these in a pan. Cut out the center of the other pastry rectangle and place it over the first one. With a fork, prick the uncovered part of the bottom layer to prevent puffing. Lightly coat the pastry with milk and sprinkle sugar on this to make it bake nicely. Place the pan in the oven at 350° until the pastry turns golden. Fill it with Chantilly cream, sprinkle with lime peel and garnish with the uchuvas.

Chantilly cream.

2 egg whites beaten until stiff
2 cups cream
Sugar to taste
1 teaspoon brandy or vanilla

Whip the cream with 2 ice cubes until wrinkles appear on the surface. Remove the ice, add the sugar and the brandy and whip again. Then fold in the egg whites.

wild blackberry mille feuilles.

1/2 lb. pastry
1/2 lb. wild berries
1 cup Chantilly cream
(p. 108)
1 cup special custard (p. 69)

Follow the same recipe used for the uchuva. Fill with both creams and garnish with the wild berries.

pastry dough.

1 lb. flour
1 lb. butter
1 cup cream
1 tablespoon salt
1 tablespoon sugar
1 whisked egg white
1 tablespoon lime juice

Spread 3/4 lb. of flour on a table. Hollow out the center and placè the salt, sugar, egg and lime juice in it. Moisten the flour with the cream and if necessary with ice water. Knead as little as possible until forming a smooth paste. Spread the dough fairly thickly, sprinkle a little flour on it and spread 1/4 lb. of butter in pats. Fold the dough in half and leave it for 10 minutes in a cool place covered with a cloth. Roll it out. Repeat this process 3 times.

tamarind parfait.

serves 12

3 egg yolks
3 egg whites beaten until stiff
1 1/2 cups sugar
Juice of 1 lime
1 cup concentrated tamarind
juice
4 envelopes unflavored
gelatine
1 cup cream

Soak the gelatine in a small amount of cold water and then dissolve it in a small amount of hot water. Beat the yolks with the sugar, then add the tamarind and lime juices. Beat until it thickens. Separately, lightly whip the cream and add to the fruit and egg mixture, then stir in the gelatine. Finally, fold in the egg whites. Spread this in an oiled pan and place it in the refrigerator. The mousse can be decorated with chocolate leaves and served with the following sauce:

tamarind sauce.

1/4 cup concentrated
tamarind juice
1/4 cup sugar
1 tablespoon lime juice
Raisins
Ginger, finely chopped
2 tablespoons Cointreau or
triple sec.

Dissolve the sugar in 1/2 cup of water and simmer until obtaining a light syrup (p. 80). Add the tamarind juice, the lime juice, the raisins and the ginger. Simmer for 5 minutes and remove from the heat. Finally, add the liqueur.

christmas cake with tropical fruits.

1 lb. of a mix of:
   Guava shells (p. 99)
   Papaya slices in syrup
   (p. 52)
   Early figs in syrup (p. 100)
   Pineapple chunks in
   syrup (p. 54)
   Raisins
   Uchuvas
   Dried prunes
1/4 lb. chopped nuts
Grated peel of 1 orange and 1
lime
Juice of 1 orange
1 lb. butter

1 lb. sugar
10 eggs
l lb. sifted flour
2 teaspoons baking powder
1/2 cup molasses
1 cup sweet red wine
4 tablespoons honey

Marinate the chopped fruits in the orange juice. Beat the egg whites until stiff, then set aside. Whip the butter with the sugar until it creamy. Add the yolks to this one by one, then fold in the egg whites. Add the fruit, the brown sugar and lastly the sifted flour and the baking powder. Lightly blend this mix. Line a cake pan with waxed paper, grease lightly and, spread the mix evenly in the pan and place it in the oven at 275° for 2 1/2 hours or until a knife stuck into the cake emerges clean. Place the cake on a dish and sprinkle the honey mixed with the wine over it.

tamarind chutney.

1 1/2 lbs. tamarind
1 1/2 lbs. guava shells, finely chopped
1 cup pineapple chunks, in syrup (p. 54)
1 1/2 cups brown sugar or
1 1/2 brown sugar loaves
1 bottle vinegar
1/2 lb. raisins
1 stick cinnamon
3 cloves
1 teaspoon salt
1 sweet red pepper, finely chopped

2 cloves garlic, finely chopped
3 small white onions, finely chopped
1 tablespoon mustard
1 teaspoon ginger, finely chopped (optional)
Salt and freshly ground pepper to taste
Hot pepper to taste

Marinate the tamarinds in vinegar. Beat them with a small chocolate beater or a whisk to loosen the pulp from the seeds, then strain, trying to obtain as much juice as possible. Mix all the ingredients and simmer for 30 minutes. Preserve in sterilized jars (p. 169).

concentrated tamarind juice.

Place the tamarind in a crockery jug, cover with water, add sugar to taste and leave overnight. Beat with a chocolate beater or wire whisk to remove all traces of pulp from the seeds and strain. This concentrate can be frozen.

tamarillos in syrup.

12 tamarillos, peeled and
with stalks
1 lb. sugar or 1 brown sugar
loaf
Juice of 3 maracuyás

Bring 1 cup of water to a boil
and dip the tamarillos in it
for 1 minute to remove their
bitter taste. Drain the fruit
and simmer in 1 cup fresh
water with the sugar for 15
or 20 minutes or until the
fruit glistens and the syrup
begins to thicken. Do not stir
because the fruit will come
apart. Allow to cool before
serving.

basic recipes for marmalade.

For each cupful of fruit, add between 3/4 cup and 1 cup of
sugar. To preserve the fruit's color and prevent crystallization
always add 1 tablespoon of lime juice.
If you are looking for a jelly-like consistency, tie the fruit's
seeds in a cheesecloth bag and leave this in the pot while the
fruit is cooking because the seeds contain pectin.

jelly.

Simmer the fruit for 10 minutes in sufficient water to keep it
covered, then blend. Leave this hanging in a cheesecloth
overnight so that the liquid can drain off. Put the liquid in a
pot with the sugar over medium heat until obtaining the
consistency of medium syrup (p. 80).

compote.

Put the fruit in the blender until it becomes smooth and then
simmer with the sugar.

marmalade.

Cut the fruit into fairly small pieces, add the sugar and
simmer.

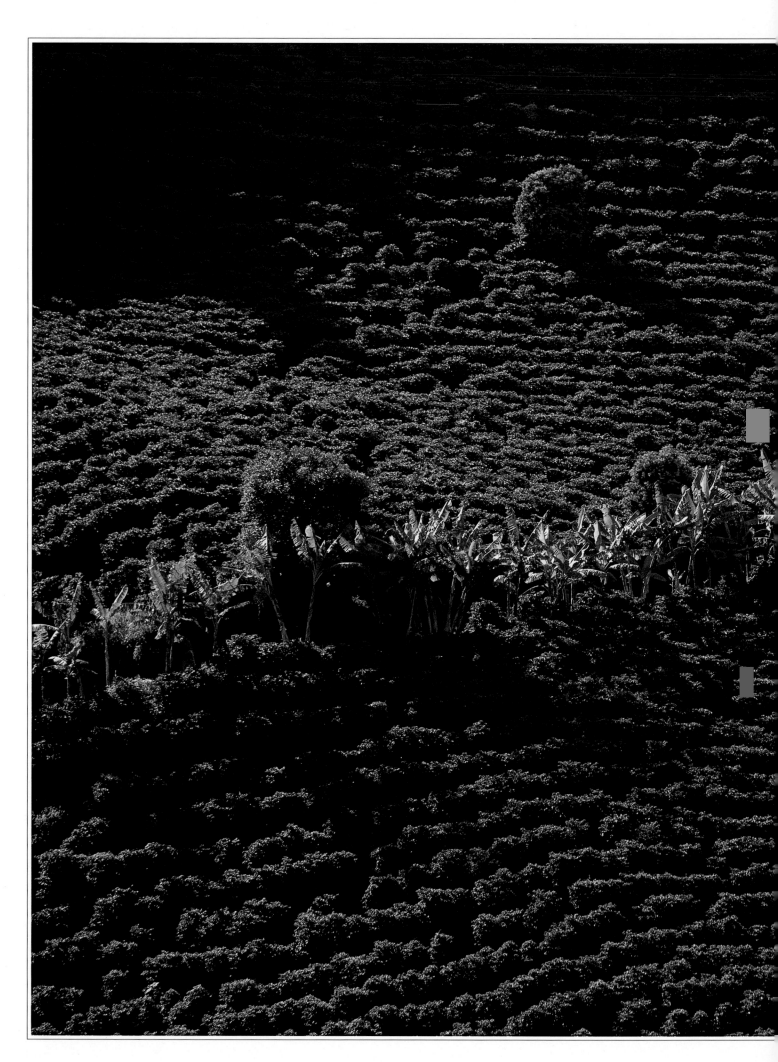

Coffee plantation with banan trees in Manizales, Caldas.

The Musaceae originally came from southeastern Asia, from regions with heavy rainfall and high humidity.

The oldest reference to them mentions India. Perhaps the wild plantain was used by mankind from the beginning of time.

In the Middle Ages, Christians called the banana "Pomum paradisi" and they believed it was the forbidden fruit with which the serpent had Eve tempt Adam. Thus, the banana was perhaps the tree of the knowledge of good and evil. Linnaeus echoed these ancient traditions by combining the Arabic name "mauz" with the modifying terms "sapientium" and "paradisiaca" to designate the first two species of Musaceae, the banana and the plantain.

Others believe that Linnaeus named the plant "muse" in homage to the renowned Italian botanist, Antonio Musa.

The plantain, larger than the banana and eaten cooked, was taken to the Canary Islands in 1402 and it traveled from there to the New World in 1516 when a Dominican friar introduced a clone to Santo Domingo. From there it spread all over the American hemisphere. The banana's original home is not nearly as well established and almost all tropical lands claim it.

The plantain clones "Sikgif" and "French Plantain" were the first to be classified in America. Among the bananas, the "Gross Michel" and "Cavendish" varieties were introduced at the beginning of the 19th century. The differences between types of plantain or banana lie in color, size, number of fingers or fruits on a stem, number of hands per bunch, color of the flowers and size of the great green leaves.

Banana

Musa sapientum L.

$\mathscr{I}$t is commonly known as banana, habano, guineo and cambur.

Numerous clones exist within the genus Musa. A clone is a type or group of types that come from one original by means of one of the procedures for asexual multiplication such as division, grafting, cutting, stem cutting, etc.

Of the Musa sapientum the following clones have been registered: banana, mysore, guayabo, guineo, baby and pygmy.

Due to its high nutritional value and creamy taste, the banana is a preferred food for babies and young children.

A fine, aromatic flour is made from the banana, superior to all others. It is slightly sweet and very nutritious, easily digested and quite appropriate for people who are debilitated, sick or recuperating from an illness.

The fruit is primarily comprised of water, carbohydrates and a certain amount of protein and fat. Banana ash is very rich in magnesium, sodium, phosphorus and nitrogen. Green bananas have more starch and less sugar than the ripened fruit. Bananas contain all of the basic elements needed by the human organism.

Bananas should be peeled and eaten immediately because they turn black quickly. They can be stored in the refrigerator; if the peel turns black, the fruit itself will not be harmed.

To choose good bananas, look for yellow fruit that is slightly green at the ends, firm but not hard. They will ripen within a couple of days.

100 g. of edible fruit contain:		
	Banana	Baby Banana
Water	74.8	69.1 g.
Protein	1.2	1.2 g.
Fat	0.1	0.1 g.
Carbohydrates	22.0.	27.4 g.
Fiber	1.0	1.5 g.
Ash	0.9	0.7 g.
Calcium	6	5 mg.
Phosphorus	25	26 mg.
Iron	0.5	0.4 mg.
Vitamin A	220	200 I.U.
Thiamine	0.04	0.04 mg.
Riboflavin	0.03	0.04 mg.
Niacin	0.7	0.5 mg.
Ascorbic Acid	10	10 mg.
Calories	84	104 cal.

Plantain

Musa paradisiaca L.

$\mathscr{T}$he plantain is also called hart and dominican.

Of the Musa paradisiaca, the following clones have been catalogued: maqueño, trucho, hartón, black, plantain's mother and liberal.

The plantain is one of the tropic's most important fruits. It is a powerful, easily digested source of nutrition. It constitutes one of the primary food staples for millions of Colombians, as well as a secondary source of income and production for coffee growers. Statistics for the regions of Greater Caldas and southeastern Antioquia indicate that there are areas where the annual per capita consumption reaches 300 kilos.

To select a good plantain, check to see that the fruit on a bunch of plantains is large and of uniform size. Each fruit should be thick in the middle, neither split or bruised nor showing any signs of insect damage. An average plantain weighs approximately 10 oz. If the plantain is too green when purchased it will whither, not maturing properly. The riper the fruit the better. The peel can turn completely black without affecting quality and it can be used just before it becomes overripe. There is no set rule, only experience can teach when a plantain is ready for each of its many uses.

The best way to store plantains is to hang one or more bunches in a cool, shady place, with the stalk if possible, so that the fruit can continue to receive nutrients. Plantains should not be exposed to cold air or wind nor stored in the refrigerator.

100 g. of edible fruit contain:		
	Ripe Plantain	Green Dominican
Water	60.8	59.7g.
Protein	1.1	1.2 g.
Fat	0.2	0.1 g.
Carbohydrates	36.3	37.4 g.
Fiber	0.6	0.7 g.
Ash	1.0	0.9 g.
Calcium	5	5 mg.
Phosphorus	30	31 mg.
Iron	0.5	0.5 mg.
Vitamin A	540	1,000 I.U.
Thiamine	0.07	0.07mg.
Riboflavin	0.03	0.03 mg.
Niacin	0.5	0.6 mg.
Ascorbic Acid	15	20 mg.
Calories	137	140 cal.

plantain soup.

serves 8

4 quarts water
2 lbs. beef short ribs
3 tender green plantains
2 lbs. potatoes, finely chopped
Salt

To make this traditional green plantain soup, make a rich broth with the short ribs. When the meat is tender, add the diced potatoes and plantain. Use your fingernail to separate the plantains into pieces to prevent blackening. Simmer until the plantains are cooked. Make a sauce from very finely chopped fresh coriander leaves and scallions. Add to this a small quantity of water, a few drops of lemon, salt and very finely chopped hot pepper to taste. Spoon this sauce over the steaming soup when serving.

banana cake.

1 1/2 cups sifted flour
1/4 cup butter
1 cup sugar
3 eggs
1 cup mashed bananas
1 teaspoon baking soda
1 teaspoon baking powder
3 tablespoons milk

Mix the flour with the baking soda and powder and set aside. Whip the butter with the sugar until creamy. Little by little, add the eggs, the bananas and the flour mix, alternating with the milk. Add a teaspoon of vanilla extract if you like. Spread this mix evenly in an greased a floured cake pan and bake in a preheated oven at 300° for 1 hour.

mareño plantains with maracuyá sauce.

serves 6

6 ripe mareño plantains
Juice of 3 maracuyás
1/4 lb. brown sugar
1/4 lb. butter
5 tablespoons honey
White cheese

Peel the plantains and place them in an ovenproof glass dish. Add all the ingredients except the cheese and bake in the oven at 375⁰ until syrupy. Remove from the oven, cut the plantains open lengthwise without severing and add the cheese. Return the dish to the oven until the cheese has melted. Serve hot.

chicken and sweet plantain casserole.

serves 6

6 potatoes, grated and fried
2 sweet, ripe plantains, diced
and fried (the skin may be
totally black)
1 can tomato paste
6 diced sausages
1/2 chicken
1/4 lb. yellow cheese, diced
Butter
6 eggs

Stew the chicken tastily in 2
cups of water, then shred it.
Dissolve the tomato paste in
the broth and leave the
shredded chicken in this.
Separately, mix all the
ingredients except the
potatoes. Lightly coat
individual casseroles with
butter and spread the
ingredients in them, breaking
an egg into each casserole.
Bake in the oven until the
egg is just done. Garnish with
the potatoes and serve.

banana pie.

Pie
Special custard (p. 69)
Chantilly cream (p. 108)
Grated lime peel
*8 sliced bananas, sautéed
in butter and, if you like,
flambéed in brandy or rum*

pie dough.

1/2 lb. butter
2 cups flour
1/2 cup sugar
1 teaspoon baking powder
1 egg
1 pinch salt

Mix all the pastry ingredients and knead them into a ball. Grease pie pan and sprinkle with flour. Place the dough in the center of the pan and spread it using the heels of your hands, lining the sides and bottom evenly. Puncture the pastry with a fork to prevent puffing, then bake it in a preheated oven at 350° for 20 or 25 minutes. One hour before serving the pie, slice the bananas, sauté them in butter and spread on the baked pastry. Cover the bananas with the custard and garnish with the Chantilly cream. Sprinkle grated lime peel and freeze for 1 hour.

baked bananas.

serves 6

9 bananas
1 tablespoon grated lime peel
1 tablespoon lime juice
2 tablespoons butter
(sugar is not necessary)

Preheat the oven to 200°.
In an ovenproof dish, put the butter, lime peel and lime juice and heat this in the oven for 2 or 3 minutes until the butter melts. Then peel the bananas, coat them with the butter and lime mix and bake them in the oven at 350° F for 30 minutes. Serve hot.

Variations: Add cream to the recipe, or serve fresh cream in a sauceboat. The bananas can also be flambéed in 1/4 cup of preheated rum.

Baked bananas are delicious served as a dessert or as an accompaniment to curry, chicken and pork dishes.

baby bananas with bacon.

serves 6

Baby bananas
6 strips bacon
Toothpicks

Wrap each tiny banana in a strip of bacon and fasten it with a toothpick. Heat a saucepan over high heat and fry the bananas, turning them until the bacon is crisp. Serve very hot.

chocolate basket with banana cream.

baskets.

1/4 lb. pure chocolate in chunks, or grated
1/4 cup vegetable oil

Line individual-sized molds (square or round ones) with doubled aluminum foil. In a pot, melt the chocolate in the oil. Pour some of this into each mold and make the liquid chocolate run onto the sides of the mold until it is fully coated, repeating the process twice. Then leave them in a cool and dry place until the chocolate hardens. Gently remove the aluminum foil.

banana cream.

serves 6

1/2 cup cream
1 tablespoon powdered sugar
1 envelope unflavored gelatine
1 teaspoon vanilla extract
3 tablespoons rum
3 mashed bananas
1/4 cup hot water

Dissolve the gelatine in the rum and add the 1/4 cup of hot water. Whip the cream, adding the sugar. Then add the banana purée and lastly the gelatine and rum mixture. Mix well and pour into the chocolate nests. Refrigerate. Serve with biscuits.

This delicious banana cream can also be used as a filling for cakes, pies, pastry shells or cream puffs.

chocolate covered baby bananas.

Baby bananas
1 can chocolate coating
Long toothpicks

Place the chocolate in a double boiler. Peel the bananas and impale them on a tooth pick. When the chocolate has melted, dip each banana in it and then stick it on a grapefruit half to dry.

fried plantains.

The principal variety of plantain is the Dominican and though it can be eaten in any of its many stages of ripeness, it should never be eaten raw.

Ripe yellow and especially blackened plantains can simply be halved lengthwise and fried in very hot oil. Drain them on paper towels to absorb as much excess oil as possible. They can also be cut diagonally in 5 inch lengths, sliced vertically into rounds or diced into small cubes before being fried. A sinfully delicious way to prepare them is to bake alternate layers of plantain, guava paste and white cheese interspersed with pats of butter and spoonfuls of cream and topped with a generous layer of beaten egg whites. Place the casserole in the oven at 350° for 15 minutes. Serve hot.

When green, peel the fruit by hand so the pulp will not blacken, cut into 1 1/2 inch thick rounds and fry in very hot oil. Remove the rounds from the frying pan before they turn golden and mash them with a big round stone or the bottom of a heavy iron skillet and then fry them again until crisp. Drain on paper towels and sprinkle lightly with salt. Serve hot. These are the famous "patacones" which are served with many regional colombian dishes. The green plantain is also delicious cut into very thin slices or rounds and fried. These intriguing crisps make a nutritious change from potato chips.

The canyon of the Central Andes Mountains, in Colombia.

Avocado

Persea americana Miller.

It appears that the avocado has existed for several thousand years. Archaeologists have found abundant remains of seeds in Mexico dating back beyond 8000 B.C. It is not known exactly when the trees were first cultivated but initially the fruit was harvested from trees growing in the wild. The Incas introduced the plant to Peru between 1450 and 1475. When the Conquistadors arrived at the beginning of the 16th century, they encountered extensive avocado groves over an immense area of the American tropics.

This fruit provides mankind with a nutritious source of food, rich in oils and proteins. In the coffee-growing areas, a plateful of beans or a rich soup are always served with slices of avocado. It is frequently used to improve salads.

Harvest times for the native avocado are May and August, while the improved species are harvested in September and December.

The avocado is a member of the laurel family. There are not varieties of avocado as much as nationalities: the round Brazilian, with sweet meat and dark green wrinkled skin; the fairly small Mexican, with a smooth thin skin, light to dark green and with very high fat content; the Guatemalan, with thick, rough and brittle skin colored dark green to blackish brown, with medium fat content; the Antillean, originally from the Sierra Nevada of Santa Marta and the most common in Colombia: a large fruit, between 1 and 2 lbs. with a long neck and thin skin colored from light green or yellow to dark green and purple.

The avocado is one of the most nourishing, healthy and digestive fruits. It partially replaces meat because of its comparable nutritional value. It contains 11 vitamins, 14 minerals as well as proteins. One avocado has approximately 280 calories. Its carbohydrate content is low and it does not contain cholesterol. It is low in sugar and sodium and the pulp has no starch. Four to 30% of the avocado is fat. Its oil is highly digestible - comparable to olive oil - and can be used for the same purposes.

To known whether an avocado is ripe or not, do not judge by the color of the skin because this differs considerably from one variety to another. However, black spots are an indication of ripeness. On gently squeezing the fruit, it should feel slightly soft. If you are not sure, stick a toothpick into the fruit near the stem and if it enters easily, the fruit is ripe. When not sufficiently ripe, the avocado has a bitter flavor.

Avocados should be stored in warm, well ventilated areas. The maturation process cannot be hurried by exposing the fruit to heat because the bitterness will persist. They can be wrapped in newspaper to aid ripening slightly.

Avocados can be kept in the refrigerator, even after having been opened, by sprinkling the exposed pulp with a few drops of lemon or lime juice, leaving the pit in place and covering or wrapping. Whole avocados cannot be frozen, but the fruit can be included in frozen soups, mousses or other preparations.

100 g. of edible fruit contain:	
Water	79.7 g.
'Protein	1.6 g.
Fat	2.0 - 13.3 g.
Carbohydrate	3.0 g.
Fiber	1.6 g.
Ash	0.8 - 5.8 g.
Calcium	10 mg.
Phosphorus	40 mg.
Iron	0.4 mg.
Vitamin A	30 I.U.
Thiamine	00.5 mg.
Riboflavin	0.12 mg.
Niacin	1.4 mg.
Ascorbic Acid	5 mg.
Calories	127 cal.

crab stick salad in avocado halves.

serves 4

2 avocados
Crab sticks
1 clove garlic
1 handful washed watercress
1 peeled and sectioned
mandarin orange
4 tablespoons salad oil
4 tablespoons orange juice
1 tablespoon fruit vinegar
1/2 teaspoon celery seeds
1/2 teaspoon oregano
4 black olives
Salt and freshly ground
pepper to taste

Set the avocados and the olives aside. Rub the garlic clove on a wooden salad bowl. Mix the remaining ingredients in the bowl. Cut the avocados in half, fill them with the salad and garnish with an olive. Serve immediately.

This is an exquisite first course for an elegant dinner or an ideal main course for a luncheon or late tea.

avocado, onion and coriander salad.

serves 6

3 peeled and tastefully sliced
avocados
1 head lettuce,
hand-shredded
2 tomatos, sliced to taste
2 red onions in fine slices

Soak the onion in salted
water for 1 hour, then drain.
Arrange the vegetables on a
platter and cover with the
following dressing:

Juice of 1/2 lime
3 tablespoons salad oil
1 small red onion, finely
chopped
1 tablespoon fresh coriander
leaves, finely chopped
1 teaspoon sugar
1 teaspoon mustard
Salt and pepper to taste

avocado, grapefruit and feijoa salad à la menthe.

serves 6

2 avocados, sliced in squares
1 grapefruit in sections,
peeled and cut into chunks
3 feijoas, sliced in wheels
1/4 lb. mushrooms, sliced
vertically
3 tomatoes, cut into cubes
1/2 sweet red pepper,
finely chopped
1/2 cucumber, peeled and
diced

Mix these ingredients in a
salad bowl and cover with the
following dressing:

Juice of 1/2 lime
2 tablespoons fruit vinegar
1 teaspoon mustard
5 tablespoons olive oil
3 tablespoons mint leaves,
finely chopped
1 teaspoon sugar
Salt and freshly ground
pepper to taste

In a cup, mix the lime juice,
vinegar, mustard, sugar, salt
and pepper. Then add the oil
and whisk by hand until
thoroughly blended. Add the
mint, marinate for 1 hour
and spoon over the salad.
Toss the salad lightly and
serve fresh.

avocado aspic.

serves 12

3 avocados
3 hardboiled eggs , separating yolks and whites
2 tablespoons cream
1 white onion, grated
2 envelopes unflavored gelatine
1 tablespoon fresh coriander leaves, chopped
Juice of 1/2 lime
Tabasco sauce
1/2 cup dry white wine
Almond oil
Salt to taste

Set the egg whites aside. Mash the avocados with a fork and add the remaining ingredients. Blend this with the lime juice. Soak the gelatine in the wine and dissolve it in 1/2 cup of very hot water, and add both ingredients to the mix. Lightly coat a mold with almond oil, spread the mix evenly in it and refrigerate. After it has set, place the aspic on a dish and garnish with the finely chopped egg whites.

breasts of chicken with Roquefort sauce.

serves 6

6 chicken breasts, boned and skinned, in halves
2 sliced avocados
Brandy
Salt and pepper

Marinate the chicken breast halves in the brandy, salt and pepper and then poach them. On a serving dish, place the chicken on top of the avocado slices, then cover with the following sauce:

Roquefort sauce.

1 avocado
Juice of 1 lime
1/2 cup sour cream
1 small white onion, finely chopped
3 tablespoons Roquefort cheese
2 tablespoons cream, lightly whipped
Salt and freshly ground pepper, to taste

Blend all the ingredients until obtaining a smooth sauce.

avocado mayonnaise.

1 ripe avocado, mashed
2 cloves garlic, peeled
1 teaspoon salt
1 teaspoon sugar
1 egg
2 teaspoons vinegar
1 teaspoon mustard
2 tablespoons lime juice
Olive or sunflower oil to taste
2 tablespoons parsley, chopped finely
Black pepper, freshly ground

Set the oil aside and blend the remaining ingredients. At low speed, add the oil in a very fine trickle until obtaining the desired consistency. Place the mayonnaise in a recipient with the avocado pit in the center to prevent oxidation. Keep in a sealed container in the refrigerator. To use, remove from the refrigerator, withdraw the pit and serve at room temperature.

Coconut

Cocos nucifera L.

$\mathscr{I}$t would appear that the coconut originated in the Pacific and then spread to the faraway islands of Oceania and to the Far East.

The tree is called the coconut palm; there are some 40 known varieties. All parts of the coconut are useful. It grows from sea level up to 4,100 ft. above sea level. Among the principal varieties are the Caribbean Giant which produces elongated and angular fruit; the Pacific Giant which has larger, rounded fruit; the Malaysian Dwarf which has multiple fruits per stalk and the Honda Dwarf which has smaller fruits.

Coconuts vary in size. A medium-sized one weighs about one pound and produces about 2 cups of shredded coconut.

Coconut is eaten fresh or shredded and toasted which enhances the slightly sweet flavor of the fruit. To make coconut milk, shred the coconut, add a very small amount of water and squeeze of coconut handfuls several times over a strainer, rinsing with the milk you obtain.

All sorts of dishes are prepared with coconut: the highly acclaimed coconut toasted rice, roasted coconut patties, custards, soups and marvelous fish dishes. Sancocho or stew made with coconut milk combines perfectly with shad. Coconut water is a very refreshing and nutritious beverage;

Cohune palm plantation in Santágueda, Caldas.

it is even claimed that coconut water curbs bad tempers. In any case, this great nut is high in carbohydrates, fats and minerals. It does, however, lose its good taste shortly after being exposed to the air, so it must be used promptly. In Colombia, when the fruit is green it is called "pipa" and is used as a drink because it contains a great deal of water and very little meat.

Non-food uses of the coconut are highly diversified. From the fibers that cover the exterior of the fruit, fishermen make baskets, fishing nets and even sails for their boats. Half of a coconut shell can be used to bail out a canoe. The fiber is also used to make brushes, mattress stuffing and even automobile upholstery, charcoal, filters and other items. From the hard, outer shell, receptacles for oil lamps are made; the wicks are made from the fiber and the oil from the fruit itself. The shell can also be made into cups, boxes, spoons; finally, it makes a luxurious veneer for fine furniture, belt buckles and buttons. Sun-dried coconut can be used to prepare glycerine, candles, balms, cosmetics, shaving cream, tooth paste and shampoo. Fiber is also used in cattle feed, and the leaf itself makes a commonly used thatch.

The outer shell should be hard, with a fibrous brown bark. On cracking open the shell, one finds liquid inside. There should be no mold around the "eyes" or black spots near the apex.

It is advisable to keep a fresh coconut in the refrigerator.

100 g. of edible fruit contain:	
Water	53.9 g.
Protein	3.6 g.
Fat	27.0 g.
Carbohydrates	10.2 g.
Fiber	4.2 g.
Ash	1.1 g.
Calcium	7 mg.
Phosphorus	80 mg.
Iron	1.3 mg.
Vitamin A	0 I.U.
Thiamine	0.05 mg.
Riboflavin	0.02 mg.
Niacin	0.5 mg.
Ascorbic Acid	5 mg.
Calories	274 cal.

Cohune nut

Scheelea butyracea Karsten.

The corozo or cohune palm is found in very hot climates between 1,500 and 2,800 ft. above sea level, growing to a height of 80 ft..

The fruit is yellow to bright orange, with a perfumed leathery skin that protects the nut.

Natives make a strong and refreshing drink from the cohune nut. The nutmeat provides fat and oil. The fruit is also used to make a delicious taffy.

The fruit is ready for harvesting when it turns red.

Chachafruto

Erythrina edulis Triana.

It is found all over the world, but it is more abundant in the tropical regions of the American continents where it thrives at altitudes of from 2,200 to 6,300 ft.

The genus Erythrina of the legume family, thus called because of the red color of its flowers, comprises 30 or more species.

Some are considered ornamental garden bushes and others are large trees that grow wild and have few industrial applications.

This beautiful, ornamental tree of variable heights grows rapidly and provides a good amount of shade. It is also widely used as a living fence post.

Chachafruto is a fruit that, cooked and eaten with salt, delights refined palates. The seeds, which look like beans, are very nourishing.

100 g. of edible fruit contain:	
Water	80.5 g.
Protein	4 g.
Fat	0.1 g.
Carbohydrates	13.3 g.
Fiber	1.0 g.
Ash	1.1 g.
Calcium	0.016 mg.
Phosphorus	0.078 mg.
Iron	0.012 mg.
Vitamin A	0 I.U.
Thiamine	0.09 mg.
Riboflavin	0.05 mg.
Niacin	0.9 mg.
Ascorbic Acid	15 mg.
Calories	100 cal.

Chontaduro

Bactris gasipaes H.B.K.

$\mathcal{I}$t prospers in hot, humid areas up to about 5,000 ft.

No classification of the varieties of chontaduro exists at present, although certain differences in the size, color and shape of the fruit itself have been noted. Its size varies, and a chontaduro can weigh from 7 to 35 oz. The color ranges from green when not ripe to bright yellow orange or ochre.

Its name derives from the Quechuan "chonta" (palm) and "ruru" or "runtu" (bone). It is borne in great bunches by tall, graceful and thorny palms, native to equatorial South America and domesticated, then cultivated by the natives, who discovered the fruit's nutritional value. The extremely hard wood from the trunk of the palm provides indigenous people with material for making lances and arrows, as well as marimbas adapted from African instruments. The taste for the peji-baye, as it is also called, slowly declined after the Conquest to the extent that it almost became an endangered species in some countries. In the Colombian Pacific, it is highly appreciated and is now being sold even on downtown street corners in major cities.

As a plant, the chontaduro has always played a part in the traditions, myths and religious beliefs of the peoples of tropical South America. Many documents refer to the harvesting of the chontaduro as an occasion for popular festivals. Among the Ticunas of the Amazon, the chontaduro or pijuayo, as they call it, is considered the palm of love, with special powers when used in engagement and wedding parties.

The fruit of the chontaduro is a complete and filling food, rich in vitamin A, with a high percentage of proteins, carbohydrates, salts, minerals and fats. It is not eaten raw but boiled, peeled and salted. Despite its food value, it is hard to digest. In some areas, it is mixed with milk, sugar and aguardiente to make a beverage similar to sabajón (an eggnog). Natives of the Colombian Pacific Coast believe that it increases fertility and for that reason, women have a high regard for it. Chonta palms bear fruit twice a year. The chontaduro's carotene content is so high that it has been recommended as an industrial source of that substance. It is one of the marvels of the American tropics.

It should be of a good size and not too hard.

100 g. edible fruit contain:	
Water	52.2 g.
Protein	3.3 g.
Fat	4.6 g.
Carbohydrate	37.6 g.
Fiber	1.4 g.
Ash	0.9 g.
Calcium	23 mg.
Phosphorus	47 mg.
Iron	0.7 mg.
Vitamin A	7,300 I.U.
Thiamine	0.04 mg.
Riboflavin	0.11 mg.
Niacin	0.9 mg.
Ascorbic Acid	20 mg.
Calories	185 cal.

Borojó

Borojoa patinoi Cuatrecasas.

$\mathcal{T}$he borojó is a 14 ft. tree that grows in the Pacific areas of the department of Chocó, where the climate is particularly hot and rainy. There, where it is commonplace and much appreciated because of its purported aphrodisiac qualities, it is used primarily to make beverages and preserves.

Drinking borojó juice sweetened with a little natural honey after exercising is very invigorating. It is one of the most nutritious of all tropical fruits. Borojó is acclaimed for its aroma. Its appearance is deceiving, even repulsive and insipid, but the flavor is exquisite. The fruit is round, about 4 inches in diameter with an opaque brown or green skin and soft, light-colored pulp which can be scooped out and stored in the refrigerator. The pulp easily turns black but that does not mean that the fruit is spoiled.

100 g. of edible fruit contain:	
Water	64.7 g.
Protein	1.1 g.
Fat	0 g.
Carbohydrate	24.7 g.
Fiber	8.3 g.
Ash	1.2 g.
Calcium	25 mg.
Phosphorus	160 mg.
Iron	1.5 mg.
Vitamin A	0 I.U.
Thiamine	0.30 mg.
Riboflavin	0.12 mg.
Niacin	2.3 mg.
Ascorbic Acid	3 mg.
Calories	93 cal.

chontaduro cream.

serves 6

12 chontaduros
2 cups milk
4 cups fine broth
1/2 teaspoon Worcestershire
sauce
1 tablespoon butter
Black pepper, freshly ground
Salt to taste

Cook the chontaduros
(p. 155), then peel and pit
them. Blend them with the
broth and then cook over low
heat, adding the milk, sauce,
pepper and salt. Simmer for
10 minutes, stirring
constantly. Add the butter
and serve steaming hot. A
teaspoon of cream can be
added to each plate of soup.

coconut soup.

1 lb. meaty soup bones
6 cups water
2 coconuts
2 tablespoons cornstarch
1/4 lb. butter
1cup milk
1/2 cup fresh cream
Salt and pepper to taste
Almonds

Make a fine broth with the
soup bones. Grate the
coconuts, including their
inner shell. Mix the coconut
with two cups of broth and
strain it repeatedly,
squeezing handfuls of coconut
to extract the milk. Return
this liquid to the broth.
In a saucepan, over low heat,
melt the butter and brown
the cornstarch, then slowly
add the milk. When the
mixture is smooth, add to the
broth, season and simmer.

Before serving, add the cream
and garnish with toasted
almonds.

chicken cha~cha~cha.

serves 4

1/2 lb. chachafrutos,
cooked and peeled
4 chicken breasts, boned
2 white onions, medium-
sized, grated
1/2 cup green pepper, finely
chopped
1/2 cup red pepper, finely
chopped
1/2 cup celery, finely chopped
3 tablespoons parsley, finely
chopped
1 cup mushrooms
1/2 cup cream

3 tablespoons butter
2 tablespoons oil
Salt and pepper to taste

Sauté chicken breasts in the oil and butter, then place them in a pot with 2 cups of water and herbs. Simmer until tender, then remove and place in an ovenproof dish with half of the chachafrutos. Sauté the onions, peppers, celery, parsley and mushrooms in butter for 5 minutes, then add the vegetables to the chicken. Blend the remaining chachafrutos with some of the broth and pour in the cream. Cover the chicken

with this. Place the dish in the oven for 20 minutes and serve hot. Garnish, if you like, with cold salted chachafrutos (p. 156).

candied chachafrutos.

1 lb. chachafrutos
1 lb. granulated sugar
2 tablespoons liquid glucose

Cover the chachafrutos with water and cook for 40 minutes or until you can easily pierce the base of the fruit with a needle. Dissolve the sugar and glucose in water and boil until obtaining light syrup. Leave the fruit covered in the syrup for 2 hours. Place the fruit and syrup in a double boiler and heat. When the syrup boils, remove the chachafrutos and allow the syrup to thicken slightly. Then cover the fruit with the syrup and leave for

12 hours. Repeat this process twice, allowing the syrup to thicken gradually. Finally, leave the fruit to dry in a large strainer in a warmdry place for 24 hours.

sea food cromeskis in Indian sauce.

serves 6

crêpe batter.

1 cup sifted flour
1 pinch salt
2 eggs
1/2 cup water
1/2 cup milk
1 tablespoon melted butter

Place all the ingredients in a blender and mix them, then leave the batter at room temperature before making the crêpes.

coconut sauce.

3 cups milk
1 bouillon cube
1 tablespoon butter
1 tablespoon Worcestershire sauce
1 1/4 cups sifted flour
2 tablespoons curry
1 1/4 cups white wine

1 tablespoon white onion, grated
2 cups coconut, freshly grated
Salt and pepper to taste

Sauté the onion in butter, dissolve the flour in the milk and add it slowly, stirring constantly and not allowing the sauce to boil. Then add the remaining ingredients and simmer for 15 minutes.

Add the following sea foods to the sauce:

1/2 cup shrimps
1/2 cup clams
1/2 cup squid, in wheels
1/4 cup sea bass
1 cup grated coconut

Mix the sea food into the sauce with a wooden spoon and simmer this for 10 minutes. Place each crêpe in a buttered pan, fill it with the sauce, then roll it and sprinkle grated coconut over it. Arrange the crêpes in the pan and bake them at 350° for about 15 minutes.

salted chontaduros.

Cook the chontaduros in
salted water for about 40
minutes or until you can
easily pierce the base of the
fruit with a needle. Peel and
serve with salt.

Variations:
Chontaduros can be cooked in
water with brown sugar or
served with honey.

salted chachafrutos.

Cook the chachafrutos in
salted water for about 40
minutes or until you can
easily pierce the base of the
fruit with a needle. Peel and
serve with salt.

coconut delights.

meringues.

3 egg whites beaten until stiff
3 tablespoons sugar
Grated coconut

Stir the sugar and the coconut into the egg whites. In an oiled pan, dab individual meringues and sprinkle grated coconut on them. Place the pan in the oven at 200° until the coconut begins to brown.

coconut sweetmeats.

1 1/2 lbs. sugar
1 grated or ground coconut
2 tablespoons cornstarch
1 cup milk
1 tablespoon butter
Powdered cinnamon

Dissolve cornstarch in milk, mix all the ingredients and simmer, without stirring, until obtaining heavy syrup (p. 80). Remove from heat, beat a little with a whisk and spoon into individual servings on a tray, garnishing with coconut shavings and cinnamon.

coconut cakes.

1 small can condensed milk
1 ground or grated coconut
1 egg
Raisins

Mix the ingredients, then spoon them into individual cakes on an oiled pan and bake at 250° until they turn golden on top.

royal crème.

This is the traditional recipe for borojó as it is served in our marketplaces. Borojó is a dark-skinned and quite aromatic fruit. A tablespoon of it adds zest to any fruit juice. Penicillin bacilli normally grow on the fruit's peel, giving it a moldy aspect, though this is not harmful to health. Simply wash the fruit in cold water. If there is a black area at the fruit's center, carefully remove it and throw it out. The rest of the pulp can be used. To prepare the sherbet, blend the following ingredients and serve immediately:

1/2 cup iced milk
3 tablespoons honey
1 cup rum
1 cup borojó
1 egg

baked fruits.

A selection of fruits
Butter
Brown sugar

Select the fruits you want and cut them into chunks, balls and wheels. Place them in a buttered ovenproof dish, sprinkle brown sugar over them and add a few pats of butter. Bake at 350° for 30 minutes.

tropical fruit fondue.

serves 4

1/4 lb. mild chocolate
1 cup milk
1/2 cup cream
Fruit in chunks

Melt the chocolate and the milk in a double boiler and then pour it into the fondue dish. Add the cream and mix well. Serve the fruit on a tray with skewers so each guest can choose a piece of fruit and dip it into the chocolate.

three Queens' salad.

serves 4

2 avocados
2 mangos
2 slices pineapple, in chunks
Juice of 1 1/2 limes

Slice open the avocados lengthwise and carefully remove their pulp, then cut this into fairly small pieces and sprinkle lime juice over it. Peel and dice the mangos and mix them with the avocado and the pineapple. Place the salad in the avocado half-shells and spoon delicious vinaigrette over it.

delicious vinaigrette.

Mix the following ingredients:

1/3 of a sweet red pepper, finely chopped
1/3 of a celery head, finely chopped
3 mushrooms, finely chopped
1 squash, finely chopped
1/3 of a carrot, finely chopped

4 leaves sorrel, finely chopped
1/2 cup lime juice
1/3 cup olive oil
Black pepper, freshly ground
Salt to taste

fruit salad parmesan.

serves 6

parmesan sauce.

1 small bottle mayonnaise
1/4 cup maraschino cherry juice
6 tablespoons grated parmesan cheese
1 teaspoon mustard

Fruits

2 mangos
3 slices pineapple
1 prickly pear
3 slices watermelon
1 small papaya
3 slices melon
Uchuvas

Peel and slice the fruit. Mix the mayonnaise with the cherry juice and 3 tablespoons of parmesan cheese. Place the fruit in a deep dish. Pour the sauce over it and sprinkle on the remaining cheese. Garnish with uchuvas and rose petals.

fruit aspic.

An aspic is a gelatine used as a salad and served with main dishes. Use the fruits of your choice.

4 envelopes unflavored gelatine
1 1/2 cups water
1 cup white wine
1 1/2 cups sugar
A selection of fruits

Soak the gelatine in 1/2 cup of cold water and then dissolve it in 1/2 cup of very hot water. Add the sugar and the wine.
Place a layer of fruit in a moistened mold, add some of the gelatine and allow it to set. Then place a second layer of fruit, add gelatine and once again allow this to set. After adding the third layer, refrigerate. Before serving, remove the aspic from the mold and garnish to taste.
Note: Keep the gelatine warm while you are making the aspic so it will not set until poured into the mold.

Homemade preserves

A larder stocked with homemade preserves is nice to have, something to be proud of, resulting as it does from an awareness of the value of healthy and natural foods. The basic advantage of preserving fruit is that you can buy a fruit in season at its lowest price and then have it available all-year-round, a not inconsiderable benefit. As you probably know, vacuum-packed fruit will not spoil for a long time.

To preserve fruit, follow this procedure:

A. Sterilize jars and lids.

Place a rack in a large pot. If you do not have a rack, place a clean cloth in the bottom of the pot to prevent the jars and lids from touching the bottom. Place the jars upside down on the grille or cloth. Fill the pot with water until it reaches the mid-point of the jars. Cover the pot and let the water boil for 10 minutes if the jars are new and for 15 minutes if they have been previously used. Remove the jars and lids from the pot only when you are going to fill them.

B. Select fruit.

Select perfectly ripe, prime quality fruit. It is important to remove any spoiled areas from each piece.

C. Wash fruit.

Carefully wash the fruit you intend to preserve.

D. Pre-cook fruit.

Blanche the fruit in boiling water and immediately soak it in cold water.

This process lets the fruit reach its final volume as well as inactivating enzymes, reducing bacteria and fixing color.

E. Fill jars.

Fill the jars with fruit to 1/2 inch beloww the top.

F. Vacuum-pack fruit.

1. Place properly-filled jars in a large pot with a rack on the bottom and fill the pot with water up to the mid-point of the jars. Boil until the contents heat up and all air is expelled.

2. Stir the preserve with a small stick to expel any remaining air bubbles.

3. It is important to wipe the edges and grooves of the jars with a warm, damp cloth to remove any traces of fruit and could let air through, and spoil the preserve.

4. Place the lids on the jars and tighten them moderately.

G. Sterilize preserves.

1. In a double boiler:
Place the covered jars in the boiler and, to prevent them from bursting, cover them with water at their same temperature to a level 1 inch above the jars. Heat the water and when it boils, cover the pot and sterilize for 2 minutes, adding 2 minutes for every 1,000 ft. above sea level.

2. In a pressure cooker:

If you use this process be careful to not fill more than 1/4 of the pressure cooker.

Syrups

H. Finish and check.

1. How to remove the jars.

Pick the jars up by their necks, not by their lids. Place them in a dry place, avoiding direct drafts. Ideally, place the jars on wood.

When the jars have cooled, clean them thoroughly and label them, specifying product and date of preservation.
2. Check the preserves.

First check after 3 hours, or when the jars have cooled, to see if they are properly vacuum-sealed. Remove the screw-bands and gently lift each jar by the sides of the lid. If it comes off, the jar was not properly vacuum-packed and it must be placed in the refrigerator and promptly consumed.

Check again on the third day, in the same manner.

Then store the preserves in a dark place to avoid decoloration. Make a third check two weeks later and a fourth one 1 month later

I. Symptoms of spoilage

Preserves which have spoiled, for whatever reason, can easily be identified by the following criteria:
a. The liquid is cloudy.
b. The color has changed.
c. The lid is puffed out.
d. You can see air bubbles produced by fermentation and the preserve, when opened, smells differently; the inside of the lid is oxidized.

J. Storage period.

Although most preserves, if properly packed, can still be good to eat more than a year later, it is best not to keep them for longer than 1 year.

*F*ruits keep very well preserved in syrup.
Many fruits can be cooked in sugar and water. A few drops of lime juice enliven the taste of the syrups thus obtained. Glucose may be added to prevent crystallization. The consistency of syrups varies:

light

Dissolve 1/2 cup of sugar in 1 cup of water and cook at moderate heat. When the syrup falls from a spoon in a continuous line, you have light syrup.

medium

Dissolve 1 cup of sugar in 1 cup of water and cook at moderate heat. When the syrup falls from a spoon as a ribbon, you have medium syrup.

heavy

Dissolve 1 1/2 cups of sugar in 1 cup of water and cook at moderate heat. When a drop of the syrup placed in cold water can be shaped into a ball with your fingers, you have heavy syrup.

caramel

Use the same proportion of sugar and water as for heavy syrup. Cook until a drop of syrup placed in cold water becomes a crystallized line.

Frozen fruits

An absolute rule: no product, once it has been thawed out, can ever be frozen again.

Natural fruit

1. Wash the fruit very well. Sprinkle lime juice on fruit that has a tendency to turn black, like bananas or apples.

2. Cut the fruit in pieces and spread these on a plate in one layer.

3. Cover the fruit with aluminum foil and freeze for 3 hours.

4. Remove from freezer, pack the fruit in plastic bags in convenient portions, then squeeze out as much air as you can and seal each bag.

5. Label and date the bags.

Freezing fruit with sugar

Place the fruit in containers or plastic bags and add 3 1/2 oz. of sugar for every 2 1/2 lbs. of fruit.

Freezing fruit with syrup

1. Place the fruit in pieces in a plastic container.

2. Cover the fruit with syrup made from 9 oz. sugar dissolved in 1 qt. cold water.

3. Seal the container, label and freeze.

To use the fruit, allow it to thaw out not long before you need it. When serving, the fruit should still be fairly cold so that it will not have softened.

Freezing juices

When a fruit is in season, its price is low and it is plentiful and of good quality, the ideal thing is to make a concentrated juice from it, adding sugar and vitamin C, if you like. Pour the juice into glasses or labelled plastic bags, then freeze it.

Properly frozen fruit can be kept up to 8 months.

Index

Bibliography

FEDERACION NACIONAL DE CAFETEROS DE COLOMBIA. Fruticultura tropical. Recopilación de las conferencias dictadas en el curso de fruticultura celebrado en el CIAT, Palmira, agosto de 1982. Ibagué, Litografía Atlas, 1985.

FEDERACION NACIONAL DE CAFETEROS DE COLOMBIA. Normas para la producción casera de Conservas de Frutas y Hortalizas. Bogotá, Departamento de Mercadeo. Sección de Tecnología de Alimentos, s.f. Folleto.

GARCIA BARRIGA, H. Flora medicinal de Colombia. Bogotá, Talleres Editoriales de la Imprenta Nacional, 1974-1975. 3 vols.

HERNANDEZ F., E. Manual práctico de cocina para la ciudad y el campo. Medellín, Félix Bedout, 1954

INSTITUTO COLOMBIANO DE BIENESTAR FAMILIAR. Tabla de composición de alimentos colombianos. Bogotá, Talleres de la Sección de Publicaciones del ICBF, 1978.

PATIÑO, V. M. Plantas cultivadas y animales domésticos en América equinoccial. Cali, Imprenta Departamental, 1969-1974. Vols. IV y VI.

PEREZ ARBELAEZ, E. Plantas útiles de Colombia. Bogotá, Litografía Arco, 1978.

POSADA SOTO, H.: Recetas de cocina de la señorita Faustina Posada Villa. Medellín, F.P.I., 1949.

ROMERO CASTAÑEDA, R. Frutas silvestres de Colombia. Bogotá, Editorial San Juan Eudes, 1961. 2 vols.

SARMIENTO GOMEZ, E. Frutas en Colombia. Bogotá, Ediciones Cultural, 1989.

TORRES, R. y RIOS, D. Frutales. Manual de asistencia técnica No. 4. Bogotá, ICA, 1980. 2 vols.